Relate, Then Educate

*The Untold Stories*
*of Teachers, by Teachers*

# Relate, *then* Educate

# Rick Holmes
# Andrea Avey

NEW YORK

LONDON • NASHVILLE • MELBOURNE • VANCOUVER

# Relate, Then Educate

## The Untold Stories of Teachers, by Teachers

Published in New York, New York, by Morgan James Publishing. Morgan James is a trademark of Morgan James, LLC. www.MorganJamesPublishing.com

Proudly distributed by Ingram Publisher Services.

**Morgan James BOGO™**

A **FREE** ebook edition is available for you or a friend with the purchase of this print book.

CLEARLY SIGN YOUR NAME ABOVE

**Instructions to claim your free ebook edition:**
1. Visit MorganJamesBOGO.com
2. Sign your name CLEARLY in the space above
3. Complete the form and submit a photo of this entire page
4. You or your friend can download the ebook to your preferred device

ISBN 9781636980744 paperback
ISBN 9781636980751 ebook
Library of Congress Control Number:
2022947931

**Cover & Interior Design by:**
Christopher Kirk
www.GFSstudio.com

Morgan James is a proud partner of Habitat for Humanity Peninsula and Greater Williamsburg. Partners in building since 2006.

Get involved today! Visit: www.morgan-james-publishing.com/giving-back

*For all the educators who have been and will be,*
*but especially those who made us who we are.*

*Gratefully and enthusiastically for Dr. Jeffrey Walker*

# Table of Contents

Notes from the Authors . . . . . . . . . . . . . . . . . . . . . . . ix

Abby French . . . . . . . . . . . . . . . . . . . . . . . . . . . . . . 1
Arturo Aviña . . . . . . . . . . . . . . . . . . . . . . . . . . . . . . 11
Shelly Swisher . . . . . . . . . . . . . . . . . . . . . . . . . . . . 21
Justin Belt . . . . . . . . . . . . . . . . . . . . . . . . . . . . . . . 33
Kelli Wilson . . . . . . . . . . . . . . . . . . . . . . . . . . . . . . 43
Rachel Whalen . . . . . . . . . . . . . . . . . . . . . . . . . . . . 51
Monte Syrie . . . . . . . . . . . . . . . . . . . . . . . . . . . . . . 61
Pam Swan . . . . . . . . . . . . . . . . . . . . . . . . . . . . . . . 71
Tonya Bobo . . . . . . . . . . . . . . . . . . . . . . . . . . . . . . 81
Carmelita Shouldis . . . . . . . . . . . . . . . . . . . . . . . . . 93

Lorena Lopez . . . . . . . . . . . . . . . . . . . . . . . . . . . . 105
Roxana Dueñas. . . . . . . . . . . . . . . . . . . . . . . . . . . 117
Amy Crawford . . . . . . . . . . . . . . . . . . . . . . . . . . . 129
Jackie Mancinelli . . . . . . . . . . . . . . . . . . . . . . . . . 141
Karen Workun . . . . . . . . . . . . . . . . . . . . . . . . . . . 153
Anna Fusco . . . . . . . . . . . . . . . . . . . . . . . . . . . . . 163

Acknowledgments . . . . . . . . . . . . . . . . . . . . . . . . . 169
About the Authors . . . . . . . . . . . . . . . . . . . . . . . . . 171
Additional Resources . . . . . . . . . . . . . . . . . . . . . . . 173

# Notes from the Authors

I didn't always know I'd be a teacher, but the signs were more evident than I would have liked to admit. My entire family is filled with various kinds of educators: superintendents, principals, counselors, teachers, school nurses, bus drivers, and more.

Outside of a couple semesters in college where I gave architecture a try, my life seemed destined to be rooted in school, a realization I was slow to embrace. I understand that what I just said hints at regret, and if I'm being honest, what you hear is correct. Let me explain.

My first attempt at teaching occurred during the student-teaching phase of my education. Up to that point, my education classes had been driven almost exclusively by course content, such as United States history, geology, and elementary statistics to name a few. To be clear, I was taught absolutely nothing about how to manage a classroom, how to connect with kids, or what to expect when I arrived at my position behind the teacher's desk.

No, up to that point in my development as an educator, I had heard only platitudes regarding the classroom and its challenges. One sentiment in particular echoes in my ears all these years later: "At the end of my first day, I walked to my car thinking, 'I can't believe I get to do this every day.'" This was said to me by a local elementary principal who had been in education for over ten years at that point.

So when I began my lesson that fateful first day, dressed in khakis and my finest collared shirt, I was woefully underprepared for what lay ahead.

I don't want this point to be lost—I was literally raised in a school. My parents, both lifetime schoolteachers and administrators, spoke of their students constantly. On an almost nightly basis, they would share stories with us about the many challenges that caring for students and their families brought my parents. These stories would regularly end with a life lesson for anyone in earshot. On most occasions, it revolved around students' innate goodness, the hardships they faced, and how discipline would provide a pathway by which they could navigate their educational career and life.

Simply by hearing these stories, being around so many teachers, and feeling the reverence for education and the lives of students, I believed I was wholly prepared for whatever might occur in my own career. Obviously, I was not.

After a lackluster stint as a student-teacher, I became a "real" teacher, holding a post at the school where I went to middle school. There are so many stories to tell about my first few years in education, but the overarching narrative could be summed up like this: "What the...? Is this how it is at every school?" Really. I asked this question, or something similar, hundreds of times in four years. It seemed impossible to me that fist fights in class, threats from a sixteen-year-old eighth grader, and vicious phone calls from parents were normal in any sense.

As it turns out, over the course of a twenty-year career in education, I found that no, it's not like this everywhere. There are better situations and worse situations to be in as a teacher. There are wonderful kids and kids who have such devastating home lives you can't reach them, no matter how big your heart is for them. There are really inspiring administrators and those that are bent on making things difficult for everyone. Of course this is true. This is true of any career.

But oh, how nice it would have been to know how diverse, beautiful, and motivating the educational landscape really is from the outset. How valuable it would have been to receive not veneered clichés or well-edited tales from Hollywood of what teaching is like, but real-life, true-grit stories straight from the mouths of veteran educators.

Such a tool of illumination did not exist when I stumbled into my educational career. If I had been able to read stories such as those contained in this book, would I still have chosen to pursue this life? Yes. Would I have been able to lift my head from my immediate troubles in the classroom, even for a moment, to see that there are immense possibilities and tools at my disposal, tools to make the outcome of my situation better for both my students and me? The answer is yes.

The book you have in your hands should be considered a powerful tool for any young educator. The stories held within are true, raw, and purposefully given without varnish. The lessons embedded in these pages are compelling and their multi-faceted applications will vary depending on the reader and the specific moment in which they find themselves. Most importantly, you will witness the vibrant heartbeat of loving teachers, which serves to inspire their students and fellow educators alike.

Frederick Douglass once said, "Some know the value of education by having it. I know its value by not having it." This proves true in my life as a teacher. The misbegotten belief that I was prepared for all the challenges of teaching when I was not nearly drove me from education after four years. Upon reflection, I understand that the inertia of my family's commitment to teaching is what allowed me to withstand the disillusionment of my early career. But how many extraordinary teachers do we lose every year because they see no lasting potential in enduring the everyday struggles?

For me, this book is an attempt to make a small deposit back into the educational profession that gave me so much. It is intended to showcase the stories of the committed souls who have chosen to jump in and equip the next generation of leaders, caretakers, protectors, intellectuals, and—yes—educators.

Enjoy.

Rick Holmes

Thank you for picking up this book. Whatever the reason you did, we believe the stories you're about to read will inspire, encourage, and comfort you. Even more so, we believe they'll level with you about the truth of teaching.

You're about to read dozens of accounts from real teachers with real stories. Each individual became an educator for a reason, and each person's purpose plays out differently in the classroom. Our hope as you move through their experiences and reflections is that you find a common thread that runs through all of us and serves to connect us.

Some people step into education after a lifelong pursuit, the inevitable fulfillment of a childhood dream. Some because they discovered a passion for it later in life or because they wanted to reach young people and make a difference. I fell into it accidentally and with great reluctance.

Young and ambitious, I was eager to do something significant after graduating from college. In my naïveté, I thought any company would be lucky to have me and jealous to do so, but for all my high ideals and lofty goals, the job market proved a cold place, completely indifferent to me. By happenstance, I was introduced to Teach for America, a program that takes nontraditional teachers and places them across the country in low-income school districts with largely underserved student populations.

I was convinced I would be a female Mr. Keating and captain my students toward honoring their hearts and chasing their destinies. Needless to say, Mr. Keating I was not, and I discovered that impacting students is earned through tears, frustration, plaguing questions, and feelings of complete inadequacy and self-doubt. *What was I thinking? Who did I think I was?* But over time, students reveal the answers to those questions. Relationships with them bring joy and affirm the mission of education. I watched as my students conquered their challenges through hard work and surprised themselves with their own capabilities.

Students will always do that, and they are deserving of our respect and effort. You'll surprise yourself as a teacher, too, by figuring things out on the fly, asking the right question in the right moment, making unexpected connections with students. But hopefully, with the help of this book and these experienced educators' stories, you'll be a bit more prepared, have a few more strategies in your back pocket, and know more clearly what it looks and feels like to be a frontline educator.

We hope you find this book helpful. And remember that no matter how difficult things get, how futile your efforts appear, or even how incredibly rewarded you feel on any given day, this work is worth it, and it matters. Because your students and the stories they are going to tell one day matter. Hopefully, this book will help you understand more clearly the role you can play in those stories and why the one you bring to the table matters just as much.

Happy learning.

Andrea Avey

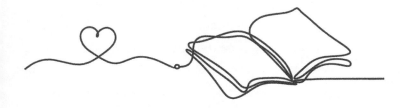

# Abby French

*Shenandoah County, Virginia*

## Moment of Impact

Have you ever felt insignificant? Invisible? Like the people around you are indifferent to your presence—even your existence?

As teachers, it's important to recognize that every student is bringing an unseen story with them into the classroom each day. Even fighting private battles at home. We may not always know the details, but we can see evidence of the struggle. When I was in my second year of teaching, I had a student like this.

Jada checked the boxes for every at-risk indicator you could think of. Broken home. Poor hygiene. Poverty. Physical abuse. Sexual abuse. She was a sixth grader. A twelve-year-old. I saw that she needed help and support, and I desperately wanted to give it to her but had no idea how. So, I did all I knew to do at the time: I made myself available.

For some reason, Jada chose me as her confidante. I could sense she felt safe with me. It was in the way we would meet one another's gaze during class. The shy smile I'd catch on her face when I'd say something silly or candid. The way she seemed to exhale stress and inhale a small bit of happiness when we'd talk. I invited her to start having lunch with me once a week in my classroom. Nothing fancy, no frills. Just an opportunity to share some undivided attention with each other over fruit and cold sandwiches.

Looking back, those lunches were some of the sweetest times for us both. As a new teacher, I felt like my good intentions were validated. It was special to share unfiltered one-on-one time with her. For me, it was a respite from the frenzy of trying to keep my head above water. For Jada, she had someone who listened to, supported, and encouraged her, someone who was there for her. She had a place of security she could go to escape the cruel eye of the cafeteria.

But in the middle of the year, all that changed.

She was taken suddenly out of school by Child Protective Services. Without warning, she was ripped from the fragile community and companionship she and I had worked so hard to forge over the school year. I was at a loss. Could I have done something more? *Should* I have done something more? Was she going to be okay? And would she and her problems be seen?

These were questions I didn't know the answers to … questions that would go unanswered for over sixteen years.

Until one day, I saw a friend request pop up on Facebook. It was Jada. She found me! After all these years, we finally connected, and she gave me the rest of her story, filled in the gaps I was missing, and reassured me that not only was she all right, but she had a daughter of her own. They were both flourishing.

Her message to me was simple: "Thank you for your kindness."

I didn't do anything special for her other than give her my time and my attention. I was a new teacher, learning and figuring things out in my own right, but I was able to offer her compassion. Dignity. Respect. Affirmation. And visibility.

She told me her self-esteem was low in middle school. She'd been shouldering a weighty burden of guilt, one she often felt she couldn't stand up underneath. She was suicidal. But because someone saw her, she was able to imagine a different path for herself. In those dark moments, our relationship made a difference to her. When she felt no one understood or cared, she could reflect on our weekly lunches, our conversations, the way we simply lived life next to each other without any sort of falsity or obligation, and that gave her hope.

Now, she writes me a letter every year. These are usually small updates, like how her daughter's doing, but she also asks me questions, mostly about parenting. She brings up things about her daughter's education. *Is this the right thing for her in this area? What about this subject and this principal in this district? Doesn't she deserve more?*

Absolutely she does.

Jada can advocate for her daughter because, in a very small way, she thinks back to how she saw me advocate for her. Our relationship allowed her to recognize she was more than her circumstances, more than a victim. She had a champion. She had someone in her corner who could see past today's problems and lend her sight to see tomorrow's potential. And now she can envision the future she wants for her daughter and can act on her behalf.

As people, it is one of our deepest desires to be seen and known and valued. It can be painful when that doesn't happen, but it can be crushing when we don't have the words to express that desire or ask for help.

Then we're all the more susceptible to those quiet little lies: *You mean nothing. No one will ever believe you. No one even knows you're hurting. How can you expect to get help, let alone escape?*

Did I have any awareness of the messages I was sending Jada when I was a twenty-two-year-old teacher? Did I understand how my small gestures were pushing back those lies that threatened to overwhelm her? Not in the least. And even now, I think, *All we did was eat lunch together.* But that's the thing about education: you never know the role you're going to play in others' stories. It is often the smallest things that have the most immeasurable impact.

Not every student can master standards. Not every student will pass those state tests come spring. But every student can be seen. Every student has a story and should get to determine how it's told. Every student can learn to view him or herself as a person of agency and power. And that is our privilege as educators—sometimes, if we see our kids that way, we can help them see the truth through our eyes. The inviolable truth that they have value simply because they exist.

## Path into Education

Have you ever felt misunderstood?

Growing up, I loved school. I possessed the early learner's enthusiasm for new information, creativity, and self-expression, eagerly looking to add to my collection of fun, new facts. Endlessly curious, I loved to learn and aimed to please my teachers.

But I failed. Over and over and over.

Despite my best efforts, I couldn't get good grades. My teachers interpreted my poor performance as apathy or laziness. The inconsistencies in my scores wreaked havoc on the reputation I wanted to build for myself: one of focus, hard work, and admiration for my teachers. Instead, the one I quickly developed was that of a classroom daydreamer: inattentive, scattered, and underachieving. As a result, school became a traumatic place I associated with struggle and an overwhelming feeling of being totally misunderstood.

My one refuge was a nature camp I attended in the Blue Ridge Mountains during the summers. This camp was legit. Dedicated to the field sciences, campers selected major and minor areas of study. We were encouraged to pursue our interests in an unbridled way, and this attitude was buoyed by the camp's nonjudgmental atmosphere.

I decided my area of emphasis would be herpetology: the study of snakes. Because, why not?

I was intrigued by snakes while everyone else was leery of them. I saw them as fascinating creatures to be studied and appreciated, though they instilled great fear in my fellow campers, and even some counselors. Because of this, it wasn't long before others came to regard me as a sort of snake expert. I could identify snakes and relocate the dangerous ones away from high-traffic areas. I learned about snakes and empathized with their plight. It wasn't their fault they were scaly, venomous, and looked frightening. So I chose to research them, even though they would have been easier for me to ignore and avoid like so many others did.

I found that the more I learned about snakes, the more the stigma around them weakened. The knowledge I was acquiring empowered me. I could look at a northern black racer and know it was harmless, while other people might assume it was a copperhead and dash off screaming. That was powerful. The knowledge I possessed was something no one could take from me, and I tried to share these insightful tidbits with my fellow campers so that they, too, could be fearless and empowered.

At the conclusion of camp, there was an end-of-term assembly where everyone celebrated the summer's memories and achievements, and a select few campers received some special recognitions. I remember thinking how mindboggling it must be to hear your name called over the microphone in front of the entire camp, how exhilarating it must feel. And then the unthinkable happened.

My name was called. I was given the award for Best All-Around Camper. I was flabbergasted. But ecstatic! Finally, people could see I really did care. They recognized how hard I worked and how deeply invested I was in the subject I'd chosen. It was with the deepest gratitude and widest smile that I received my award.

If only my teachers and classmates at school could see me the way the counselors and other campers saw me.

When I went back to school, the chasm between the true desires of my heart and my performance in the classroom was vast. For the life of me, I still couldn't understand what was going on, and no one around me seemed to grasp my dilemma either.

Then came sixth grade. When I was eleven years old, I was diagnosed with a learning disability. We discovered I had auditory limitations, processing issues, and challenges with short-term memory. What my teachers had always chalked up to laziness and not listening was actually an inability to hear them properly. What seemed, on the surface, a blatant lack of preparation on tests really was a roadblock in my short-term memory center. At last, people knew I wasn't blowing off my schoolwork or allowing my attention to wander from the classroom. At last, I was seen rightly for who I was. But gosh, if it had only happened sooner.

Today, it is my honor and my duty to help students figure out who they are. If they are struggling, I want to help them. If they are at odds with the coursework, I want to get to the bottom of the issue and problem-solve together. If they feel invisible, I want to make them feel seen. If they feel misunderstood, I will work to understand them.

To this day, I keep my Best All-Around Camper award on my dresser. Looking at it every day reminds me that I have been seen and understood. It is the manifestation of being known, and it spurs me on to help students define their worth and see themselves as valuable.

I teach to empower others with knowledge. I teach because information is the solvent to fear. I teach because ignorance breeds ignorance, and education breeds empathy. I teach because I see myself—that misunderstood eleven-year-old who needed an advocate—in my students. It is my purpose to reflect their power back to them, so they can feel it, own it, and use it.

## Best Practice

*"I could sense she felt safe with me. [. . .] I invited her to start having lunch with me once a week in my classroom. Nothing fancy, no frills. We just shared some undivided attention with each other over fruit and cold sandwiches."*

More informal settings can be great ways to develop and deepen relationships with students. This could be in the context of a sport, club, or other extracurricular activity. These moments are invaluable in getting a glimpse of who students are as truly complex individuals beyond their basic performance in your class. On the flip side, this is an opportunity for students to get to know you as more than "just a teacher." Maybe even as a real human being. But what if you're not on any coaching staff or sponsoring any school organizations?

One idea to get more casual time with students is to invite them to have lunch with you in the classroom. Now, this is something in which you need to exercise discretion and your best judgment. We recommend these lunches always occur with the classroom door open and not between students and teachers of opposite gender. Meeting with small student groups of two and three is even better and less intimidating than a one-on-one lunch. Keep the conversation light and relaxed and let the student(s) lead. Consider what an appropriate cadence could be. Weekly? Monthly? Use discernment, and never put a student (or yourself) in an uncomfortable or unseemly situation. Discuss your idea with a veteran teacher in your school before initiating something like this. You want to be aware of the school's culture and policies regarding student-teacher interaction outside of designated class time.

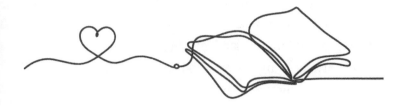

# Arturo Aviña
*Los Angeles, California*

## Moment of Impact

Children don't put up any sort of facade, and what you see is what you get. After existing solely in the world of adults, this truth is uncommon and deeply refreshing. When thinking about a career, I always knew I wanted to be around kids' energy, do my best to influence them for good, and experience life through their eyes, but I wasn't sure how that would play out in my life.

Once I graduated from college, I began work as a mentor-program coordinator to try out the school setting and get a feel for that context, and once I did, it was obvious that education was the right fit for me. I earned my education credentials, and my first teaching job was in kindergarten. At my new school, it was tradition for the kindergarten classes to perform a play and a few songs at the end-of-year culmination. As someone who had always leaned toward the science and math disciplines during college, I was nervous. I felt out of my depth with the arts, and I had no theatre experience to speak of. But, as it turned out, I loved it! That first year was a fabulous experience, so by the next spring, I was ready and eager to put up our little show. Allowing my kids to do something fun, exciting, and outside of our regular routine was a year-end treat, and this quickly became the highlight of each year. I even started an after-school drama club because I enjoyed it so much and my students wanted a bigger outlet for the performing arts.

Eight years into my educational career, I felt I was hitting my stride. I had carved an unexpected niche for myself in the arts and was running with these yearly performances. My students and I were having the greatest time each spring brainstorming ideas and sharing them with the broader school community. In spite of the budget cuts my school was suffering, we kept up this wonderful tradition, which I was grateful for. The arts are powerful, and I wanted to do all I could to keep that space alive and thriving for my kids. However, our beautiful bubble was about to be punctured.

While our drama club and yearly performances had escaped the threat of being cut, I hadn't. I received a pink slip in March, signifying I was in danger of being let go at the end of the school term due to a lack of funding.

Although this was a blow, especially as I was feeling so established and settled in my profession and at my site, it's an unfortunate reality for too many educators in our country. Initially, I felt angry and slighted and was tempted to check out for the rest of the year. But once I had a little time to process the news and recalibrate my perspective, I realized this was in no way my kids' fault. They shouldn't bear the brunt of my district's issues or my administration's decisions. With all the uncertainty facing me, I decided to make the most of my time while I had it. I decided that if this was really going to be my last year teaching, I wanted to go out with a bang, so I poured all my passion, energy, and time into the end-of-year performance with my students.

Typically, the songs performed for kindergarten culmination were what you would expect five-year-olds to sing. Simple, kid-friendly, neutral. But that wasn't how I wanted to cap off my potential last year with my students. I wanted to make a memory that would last. I wanted to pull off something surprising, bold, and unforgettable.

I taught my students a choreographed routine to Madonna's "Vogue."

My kids loved it! Their *parents* loved it! This was something completely unusual and new, and it invigorated all of us, especially my students. Doing the choreography and singing to such an iconic song was something my kiddos had never done before, but we had a sensational time. With permission, I posted the performance, and it actually went viral, which was not something I'd intended, but what a special way to celebrate and share this achievement of my students. Plus, for me personally, that performance became the reaffirmation I needed at a very low point in my career. The doubt that had begun to creep over me after receiving that pink slip completely diffused during this period with my students. The perception I was battling of myself as a dispensable faculty member, someone who wasn't making a difference or wasn't worth keeping around, changed. This experience with my students, the risk we took together, and the rewarding moments of joy and validation helped me see myself accurately once again.

Thankfully, that pink slip was rescinded, and I was able to stay at my site. Of course, I felt immense relief, but I recognized I had also gained a renewed sense of creativity and urgency as an educator. The threat of losing my job had hung over me, weighing heavily on my heart as I tried to consider and plan for the future. Conversely, it had also liberated me. I stepped into a freedom in the classroom I hadn't had before, one I likely wouldn't have accessed if

I had felt more assured in my prospects. With the future dangling loosely before me, I had nothing to lose, and as a result, I discovered and gained so much more.

Now that I knew I could continue teaching, I decided to carry this new attitude of daring with me. For the Madonna performance, I bought a video camera to record my incredible students, so now I had a new piece of equipment to utilize in the future. Suddenly, completely new possibilities opened to me. There was so much untouched territory I wanted to explore with my students. No way were we going back now. I wanted to continue to take risks and be bold. I sought out-of-the-box ideas and approaches. Because my students and their families loved the "Vogue" experience, my classes started making music videos and experimenting with other performance methods and formats.

This sort of music-driven performance is the essence of what a lot of my classes do now, especially in drama club and our other performing arts ventures. I've been making videos like this with my students going on eight years now, and it's staggering to consider that all these incredible memories stem from one risky decision, one "accidental" success. One pink slip.

## Path into Education

The idea of legacy is sewn into the fabric of education. The whole aim of education is to impart lessons, skills, and memories to students in the hope that they will remember and leverage them to achieve success, make a difference, or create the life of their dreams. Educators often view the process of instruction this way: we give something to students, students take it, and they benefit from it somehow later on. It's no stretch to believe a particular academic concept or habit will serve a student well years into the future. What's harder to comprehend is the idea that generations of educators and students are telling a single story, each contributing new chapters to a single narrative, however many years apart that may occur.

I think that's what's happening with Mrs. Saville and me.

In elementary school, I was a pretty shy kid. I kept to myself most of the time, and taking risks and being super outgoing were not my things. Mrs. Saville knew that about me. She saw beyond my quiet exterior and introverted tendencies. When I think of what a "best teacher" looks like, she comes to mind. She was gentle and kind, playful and supportive, helpful and humorous. She gave her students opportunities to learn, grow, and step out of the boxes we had placed ourselves inside of. We trusted her and she made us feel secure; we knew we could survive being uncomfortable, even if only for a little bit, because she was there to keep us safe.

In fifth grade, Mrs. Saville had us make a class film as part of the D.A.R.E. initiative in my school. As a reserved student, I never would have volunteered to perform in it on my own, preferring instead to contribute in some other way. But I was a good student, and Mrs. Saville—believing I would rise to the occasion—cast me in the film. I look back and laugh when I think of the role I was assigned: a special detective searching for drug addicts. I know, right? Like, *what*? But yeah, that was the character I was given. It was a relatively small part, which was fine with me, but I did my best with it, and even in my minor role, Mrs. Saville made me feel like a star. She gave me a chance to try something different, to dip my toe in the water and see how it felt, and she was so proud of me for breaking open my shell by playing this goofy kid detective. After that, I wasn't so scared or timid anymore. It wasn't an overnight transformation, but some of the fear dissolved, and I learned I was capable of more than I thought. Plus, I realized performing wasn't scary. Actually, it was pretty fun.

When it was time to think about college and my future career, I gravitated toward work involving kids. A fan of science, I studied psychology and was really interested in becoming a child psychologist. However, I soon figured out I wasn't interested enough to earn a master's degree, and once I got a taste of being in a classroom, that was it for me. I became an elementary teacher. I ended up teaching in my hometown at the school I'd attended myself as an elementary student, and while that déjà vu experience has its weird moments, I really love it. It feels like home. I recognize neighbors, see my students' families walking in the area, and even work alongside some of my former teachers. My school is a special place, with so much of my history housed in this little building.

As I began to etch my imprint on the school as an educator, I was drawn to the performing arts, much to my surprise. My strengths had always been firmly rooted in science and logic. Up to this point, I believed the creative and performing arts were incompatible with my abilities, but, like muscle memory, I thought back to fifth grade and remembered my positive experience of trying something new. When I directed my class in the school's year-end singing and dancing culmination event, I fell in love with performance again, and I could see the freedom and joy I felt mirrored back to me in my students. These performances evolved into the pinnacle of the school year for me, and drama and music began to saturate my instructional practices more and more. Now, I'm dedicated to the arts full time, and I think a lot about Mrs. Saville. I do my best to channel her energy and emulate her kindness as much as I can. I try to provide the same incredible memories and opportunities for my students that Mrs. Saville gave me.

Sometimes, our stories aren't the ones we imagine writing for ourselves.

When I reflect on little fifth-grade Arturo, a shy nerd who cared so much about his schoolwork, it's almost impossible to recognize him in who I've become, an arts-education specialist working with a variety of schools in the Los Angeles area. But thinking back on where I've been and all the potential I possess reminds me that the same truth applies to students. No one stays static. Children grow and change and try out different versions of themselves. I'm so thankful I had an exceptional educator to act as my safety net. If it weren't for Mrs. Saville, I truly don't know where or who I would be today. The line leading from then to now is just so clear.

Mrs. Saville put me in that class film when I was in fifth grade. I became a teacher, like her, and I began to create films with my students. I would see students and give them roles in productions. I would see them light up with that flicker of self-awareness and pride, and now I'm working in the theatre arts exclusively. It's wild.

Mrs. Saville will always be a part of my story, and I am a continuation of hers. I am one of many offshoots of her legacy, and I get to tell her story year after year every time I support a drama club, watch my kids in a performance, or step into a classroom to serve and celebrate students. Now, my students are a part of her story, as well as mine, and are benefitting from her legacy. Our stories are really all the same: just distinct strands braided into the same rope.

## Best Practice

*"[A run-of-the-mill performance] wasn't how I wanted to cap off my potential last year with my students. I wanted to make a memory that would last. I wanted to pull off something surprising, bold, and unforgettable."*

Teachers' manuals and pacing guides are just that: instructional supports and frameworks for the year. They are signposts to help you gauge how to get where you're going in one academic year. These resources are helpful, but they shouldn't trump the needs of your students or the distinct spark that distinguishes you as an educator. If you're bored, your students are, too, and the time is ripe for reinvigoration. Creativity and excitement in the classroom enrich instruction and are valid additives to help students remember standards and objectives. It's important to be your unique self as an educator. If you aren't, both you and your students are missing out.

What is a lesson or unit that could use a new approach? Think about a lesson plan you've done over and over that's losing its potency. How can you brainstorm new ideas with your students? What particular traits or interests of yours can you apply to your instructional methods to make learning more fun for you and your class?

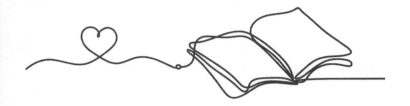

# Shelly Swisher
*Mesa, Arizona*

## Moment of Impact

"They won't care how much you know until they know how much you care."

If you're in education, you've heard this idea or some version of it thrown around. Likely *ad nauseam*. Clichéd or not, this isn't an empty phrase. It's a fact.

For me, being known and understood by one of my English teachers, Mrs. Wilkie, changed the course of my life. She not only saw who I was but also who I could be. In my own classroom, I try to do the same thing for my students.

Classroom culture is paramount to me. Relationships are the cornerstone of safety and growth, and creating a protected space for students is one of my first priorities each fall. I want students to feel secure enough to be themselves with me and with each other. This richness of relationship adds a layer of safeguarding around our classroom discussions. It provides a freedom for us to talk through difficult topics, confront hard questions, and stretch into respecting one another in new ways.

My first year teaching, I had three different classes to prepare for, a six-month-old, and the responsibility of being the cheer sponsor. Even with such a full plate, I sweated the small stuff. I agonized over details, rehashed offhand comments made by students or parents, scrutinized my lesson plans, and reached for perfection in unsustainable ways. Thankfully, over time, I relaxed into teaching and grew more comfortable in my profession, which enabled me to let go of some of that small stuff and realize it pales in comparison to meatier matters, like authenticity in the classroom.

One of my favorite ways to work toward deep relationships with kids is an activity I have them complete at the beginning of each school year. I pass out a little questionnaire to every student, asking them to list all their hobbies, interests, and extracurricular activities. It's important to me to get to know my students as soon as possible, and this list is an invaluable resource in service of that goal. But I don't stop there.

I look over the things my students list on their information sheets and make a point of attending one game, performance, match, concert, whatever for each student at least once in the year. While I'm there, I do my best to make my presence known to the student. I've had wonderful moments at these events over the years. Outside of the physical space of the classroom, a veil falls, and the distance between student and teacher shortens. I have no red pen in hand. I'm not assigning homework. Here, there are no rules of mine to loom over a student. It is their space, not mine. They are in their natural environment, having fun with their classmates and often doing something they enjoy and maybe even excel at. The scale tips in the student's favor, and I am delighted to be a spectating fan instead of a presiding authority.

Over the years, as I have prioritized this connection beyond the classroom, I've met parents, celebrated student successes, laughed off mistakes, and commiserated over losses. I've had the opportunity to peel back some of my students' layers, and they've had the chance to do the same with me. We're all human, and nobody is one-dimensional. Seeing students outside of the classroom context helps me expand my picture of who they are and opens my eyes to who they could become.

Knowing facts on paper is only one aspect of really knowing a student. I also make a concerted effort to know what's going on in their lives beyond school walls. I want to know if a student's parents are divorcing, if they have a loved one with a serious illness, or if they have battled any mental-health issues. While these are details I don't ask for on a get-to-know-you sheet, they are tidbits I pick up on through sincere conversation, asking meaningful questions, and paying attention to students' behavior and moods. Being aware of these important parts of students' lives helps me better understand, support, and serve them. These are things every educator wants to do for their students, but it can be scary to make yourself vulnerable and stick your neck out for your kids. But those moments are often the most impactful. I've seen this in a small way myself.

One day in class, my students were engaged in a discussion activity. Everyone was out of their seats, milling around, and we were talking through the themes present in our current text of study. Students expressed opposing points of view and responded to their classmates' opinions. In the course of conversation, one student, Kyle, was debating another student's perspective and referred to the student, someone who identified as transgender, with inaccurate pronouns. Students' nervous eyes flicked back and forth between Kyle, me, and the student in question, Sydney.

For a moment, I felt paralyzed. I had a choice to make: to address Kyle's remark and correct his language or not. In this case, he used masculine pronouns when Sydney had made it very clear she used the pronouns of *she*, *her*, and *hers* to describe herself. It was a small moment, but it held great potential for impact, for better or for worse. If I really wanted to be a teacher who took knowing her students seriously and who was willing to step into the line of fire for them, that meant I had to be bold and actually take that step.

I seized the moment and spoke to my class.

"Let's pause for a second. I want to remind everyone that Sydney uses 'she' and 'her' pronouns and has asked us to do the same. We all want to be respected and valued for who we are, so let's be careful how we speak and be sure to interact with one another accurately and considerately."

Students know when you go out of your way to acknowledge who they are, whether it's a recognition of something small, like the instrument they play in the school band, or something of profound significance, like their gender identity. The school years are formative for students, and it's always the right choice to encourage and bolster them as they grapple with who they are and shape their identity and future.

Everything gets better when a student feels safe and valued—student performance, rapport, classroom management. I can't remember the last time I wrote a behavior referral, and I attribute that to the fact that my kids know I truly care about them. That care is formed over time, made up of moment after moment of wishing them happy birthday, knowing their sports schedule, greeting them in the hall, and holding a safety net underneath them when they venture out boldly. Genuine student relationships are the root that, when cultivated, leads to a healthy, whole, and enjoyable classroom experience.

## Path into Education

Teaching has been in my bones since I was a child. It's a desire I remember always being there, something I never wondered about or questioned. You never ask your heart to beat or lungs to expand and release. They just do. They simply *are*.

I come from an uneducated family. Literacy among my family members was exceedingly low, if it existed at all. My grandparents on my mom's side had elementary levels of education. When I was young, I remember my grandpa signed his name with a simple X, and if a true signature was required, it was my mom or my uncles who signed on his behalf. I remember thinking this was a curious thing for my grandpa to do, not fully understanding what was really going on. When I was in fifth or sixth grade, I grasped the truth and tried on my teaching hat for the first time: I taught my grandpa how to write his name. Just like that, I had my first student.

In light of my background and the examples I saw in my family, I thought my educational road ended at high school. College was not a prospect I considered. No one else in my family had gone, so neither would I. Mine was a path I never viewed as changeable. That's how things had been for everyone else, so why should they be any different for me?

Because Mrs. Wilkie came along and changed my trajectory.

She was my sophomore English teacher, and her daughter was one of my good friends. I knew her in that special way you know your friends' parents: in casual conversations while getting ready for bed, through drives in the car to and from each other's houses, over chats at dinnertime when you used their plates and cutlery like one of their own.

She saw something for me I didn't: a different path.

With Mrs. Wilkie in my corner, I started thinking about college for the first time in my life. Suddenly, when I imagined my future, unexplored options rose up in my mind, and whole new avenues I hadn't been aware of before presented themselves to me. This was exciting yet confusing. I saw there was another path I could take, but I had no idea how to get there. Without anyone in my family who had walked that road themselves, I wasn't very well equipped to navigate, let alone begin, the college application process. I needed a guide. That's where Mrs. Wilkie stepped in.

As a first-generation university student, I didn't know where to start, but Mrs. Wilkie was there every step of the journey. After planting the seed in my mind, she didn't just wish me well and watch my progress from afar. She helped me organize application materials, track deadlines and recommendations, and even apply for financial aid. When I was accepted, she's the one who took me to enroll in classes on campus. I became a college student, and a college graduate, because of her.

Now, I am a teacher because of her, too.

Of the thirty years I have spent teaching, I taught sophomore English for fifteen of them. Like she did. As I look back on my career so far, I see one continuous thread unspooling all the way from Mrs. Wilkie. It was her care for me and her remarkable efforts, completely above and beyond, that showed me I could change my story. I wasn't alone. I had the power and agency to alter my course, and not just in small ways but in very large, monumental, life-changing ways. She showed me what I was capable of. Her unwavering support for me and her clear-eyed vision of my potential carried me through my senior year, and now that I'm on the other side of that experience, I remember the impact these qualities of hers had on me and I try to exhibit them toward my students.

Every young person needs that one adult in their lives who says, "I believe in you. You can do this." I think if we look back on our lives, we can all acknowledge the influence this sort of encouragement, or its lack, had on us. The world is changing rapidly, and it feels like the ground keeps shifting so drastically that young people can't even find their footing. An established, empathetic adult can help.

A lot of my students over the years have come from loving families, but it's not uncommon for parents to be away from the home often, working multiple jobs to provide for their children, going to night school, or balancing some other responsibility or obligation. As a teacher, I have the opportunity to be that One Adult for my students. Every day, I consider how I can show my kids they matter. How can I create safety for the students in my classroom? How can I build their confidence? How can I show up for them and remind them that they are capable of more than they might think? How can I help them realize they have the power to write the story they want for themselves?

When I was honored as Teacher of the Year in my district, I could invite ten guests to sit at my table for the ceremony. Mrs. Wilkie was one of them. While ostensibly I was the guest of honor, I couldn't help but view that evening, spent with Mrs. Wilkie by my side, as a way of celebrating her incredible work, too. I am who I am as a person and an educator in so many ways because of her, and I am so grateful she saw an alternative future I could not.

We rarely get full-circle moments in life, but when they come along, especially in education, they really blow your mind. While I always wanted to be a teacher growing up, I had no idea how I would get there until Mrs. Wilkie showed me the way. She was the One Adult in my life that not only believed in me but also handed me the tools I needed so I could help myself. Because of her immeasurable legacy in my life, I enter my classroom each day knowing I am privileged with the opportunity to be an advocate and ally for my students. Whether I will be or not is something I may never know, but if I am? Well, that's priceless.

All it takes is one.

## Best Practice

*"I pass out a little questionnaire to every student, asking them to list out all of their hobbies, interests, and extra-curricular activities. It's important to me to get to know my students as soon as possible, and this list is an invaluable resource in service of that goal."*

Culture-building activities are likely a part of your start-of-year practice. If you don't use a resource like Shelly's, consider creating a get-to-know-you sheet and allotting class time for students to complete it. Ask questions about students' interests outside of school, their birthdays, families, favorite movies, anything. Read their responses and remember them. Ask follow-up questions and tell them "Happy birthday" when it's their day. Such intangible details go a long way in making genuine connections with students.

But don't stop there. Like Shelly, commit to attend one extracurricular event per student per school year. Go out of your way to make contact with your student(s) during the event if possible, and after the fact, let them know you were present and cheered them on. Comment on how fire their flute solo was or how they were robbed of that charge in the fourth quarter. Celebrate them and honor who they are as complex, nuanced individuals.

This is a practical way for you and your students to dismantle any preconceived notions you may have of each other. This is especially relevant in small schools or if your students stay in the same building for several years before they reach you. The relationships you'll build with students will make the effort more than worthwhile, and you might have the same experience as Shelly in seeing behavior issues, classroom disruptions, and negative attitudes simply disappear.

If you already have an intro activity like this, revisit it and set a goal to start attending student activities this month. If you don't have something like this questionnaire in your repertoire, make space for it in your current unit and start carving out time to support your students. Who will be first on your list?

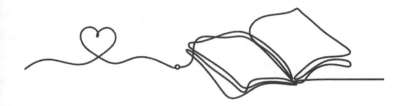

# Justin Belt

*Carrollton, Texas*

## Moment of Impact

Shawn's fists did the talking for him. He didn't know how to express the emotions welling up inside of him. His anger and frustration knew no articulation, an elusive foreign language he wasn't fluent in yet. He opted instead for the quickest, easiest means of communication—force.

I was teaching eighth-grade English. At the time, I was making it a point to invite students to have lunch with me in my classroom. One of those students was

Shawn. During one of our lunches, I brought up his behavior. I never had any issues with him in my class, so I was curious to understand why he was quick to conflict elsewhere. He told me that all he knew was aggression and getting physical. I encouraged him the best I could.

"You know, you have the power to filter these emotions. You don't have to fight just because that's what you're used to. You're smarter than that. You *can* overcome this."

I didn't think I'd gotten anywhere with him. He nodded his assent, shrugged off our conversation, and then moved on when the bell rang signaling the end of lunch.

Shortly after that day, there was an incident and Shawn didn't talk to me for the remainder of the year. Since I was teaching eighth grade, my students moved out of the building as they progressed to high school. I didn't see Shawn anymore and was left wondering how things were going during his freshman year. And then one day, I was on site at the high school for an interview. I was waiting on a bench in the hallway, thinking over potential questions and prepping myself for the meeting.

*"Mr. Belt!"*

I looked up, startled off my mental game, and saw Shawn. He came running down the hall and plopped down on the bench beside me as if no time had passed.

"Hey, Mr. Belt. I want you to know I haven't gotten in any trouble so far this year!" He laughed, and so did I. He was smiling, and so was I.

"Man, that's great! I knew you had it in you. I'm glad to hear it," I told him. And then he darted off just as quickly as he'd come. I was left on the bench with my own whirlwind of emotions to sort through: relief to finally know how things were going for him, happiness that he was off to a good start and keeping a level head, but also disorientation at having been so disarmed by our encounter. How was I going to get my head right for the interview *now*?

When I think about our lunchtime conversation all those years ago, I'm still surprised at the impact my words had. As teachers, we hope we're planting seeds every day with our students. But you can never be sure if those seeds will take, if the soil you're planting in is ready to receive them or not. But you'll never know if you don't try, and no opportunity is to be wasted.

Having taken a circuitous route into education, I'd seen professionals do a lot of things well and even more things poorly. When I finally got into the classroom, I resolved to learn from others' bad examples, so I knew I was going to prioritize relationships with my kids. One of my longstanding convictions is that my primary job isn't to help kids identify misplaced modifiers or analyze Shakespeare's dramatic structure—it's to help them become the best human beings they can be. What the world really needs, and what we're all banking on if we actually think about the future, is a kinder and more compassionate human race. So, as an educator, I create and seize as many opportunities as I can to help my students walk in that direction.

There are so many factors that affect kids. Everybody's got baggage, and our students are no different. It's completely ridiculous to write them off just because they're young. If anything, that makes them more deserving of grace and their burdens all the more serious.

Meeting students where they are is more than just adding in remediation as you help them on the road to mastery. It's about really seeing them in the midst of their struggles and staying by their side. It's helping them identify what they're up against, equipping them to overcome it, celebrating with them when they succeed, and encouraging them when they have to try again.

At any moment, the words you say could lodge their way into the heart of a student with the power to help or hinder. The decisions kids make could be the catalyst for generational change in their families. One pivotal moment with a student could result in them becoming a first-generation college student or proceeding down a particular career path. Heck, even leading them toward a career at all!

While I haven't seen Shawn since his surprise appearance before my interview, and I don't know where he is now or what's become of his old habits, I do know that one bit of my advice helped him in some way at least once. Sometimes, that's all we get. We're presented with moments and students, and it's up to us to grab those opportunities and make the most of them.

## Path into Education

There are some things that are just in your blood. Habits that run in your family, skills passed down through generations thanks to genetics, legacies handed off from one family member to another.

For me, there was *no way* that thing was going to be teaching.

I hailed from a long line of educators: my grandmother, both of my parents, both of my sisters. You might think that being around teachers like this would endear me to the profession, inflaming a warmth in my heart for it after so many years of close proximity. It didn't.

In fact, it had the opposite effect.

Growing up with educators for parents, I saw the nitty gritty of what being a teacher was really like. The long hours, the thankless efforts, the endless stream of grading, the parent-teacher conferences, the "voluntary" chaperoning at countless dances, football games, talent shows, field trips, theatre rehearsals, debate team meetings. The list goes on and on.

I didn't want that life for myself. To me, teaching looked like an extremely tough job with little to no payoff. It's no secret that educators' salaries are laughable, and all the stress and extra work seemed too high a price to pay to enter a profession, albeit one as noble as education. So I decided to pursue my passions: music and vocal performance. Upon graduation, I was entertaining two job offers, an ideal situation for any fresh college grad, but I turned them both down. They were teaching gigs, and I didn't want to be a teacher. So I went back to the drawing board and became a human resources manager, a role I had for seven years.

Initially, this job was one I enjoyed. I supported and guided adults in their professional careers so they could define the best path for themselves. But over time, it began to wear on me. It wasn't the most thrilling or fulfilling job, a truth underscored by the fact that my wife had a job she was consistently excited about. The contrast between my feelings and hers was tough to stomach day in and day out. I grew more and more weary of my daily grind, slower to get out of bed with each passing morning. My wife, however, woke up eager to head to work and make a difference, connect with people, and draw upon her expertise.

She was a teacher. *Of course* she was a teacher…

Yet she was filled with joy. She looked forward to doing her job, even on her hardest days, while I didn't. Eventually, it became evident that the time was right for me to make a change. I was ready for something new and refreshing. Something more meaningful. So I resigned from my HR post. As I considered what might be next, I ultimately recognized I needed to take a chance on what had been tapping me on the shoulder my whole life: education.

Once more, I returned to school ... this time to become an educator. I started out as a library assistant at an elementary school, and the joy and pure emotion of my students was the most reviving drink of cold water after a long season of drought. Seeing their faces light up every day rejuvenated my spirits and awakened parts of me I hadn't even realized were dormant. I sensed I was on the right track, but it wasn't until I started substitute teaching in middle-school classes that I was sold.

Middle schoolers are my people! They get it. They're funny, unfiltered, challenging, and hungry—hungry for truth, for a champion, for authenticity, for the realness of life, for the tools to mature and improve themselves. I loved my time as a sub with that age group, and I knew I'd found what I'd been looking for in a career all this time. Teaching was something I couldn't escape; I could only delay it. So I went all in and became an eighth-grade English teacher, and I now know without a doubt teaching is my calling. I am here on this earth to encourage, inspire, and motivate students. I want to make an impact.

There are some things that are just part of your story. Things like the passion you can't seem to shake or that idea that hangs in the back of your mind persistently. It's the voice that reverberates throughout your life's narrative, leaving clues as you move from decision to decision, whispering to you all the while.

For me, that thing is teaching.

## Best Practice

*"About four years ago, I was teaching a unit on mood and tone, and students were having a hard time understanding. So I pulled out my guitar, and in that moment, I made up a song about my mood. I sang that I was angry with myself because I couldn't help my students understand the lesson. I started strumming hard, like a rock anthem. My students noticed my anger, and I asked, 'Anger is my what?' Mood. 'Okay, you've identified my mood. Describe to me your mood, and let's write a song together to illustrate it and how it might sound.' Next class, we scaffolded up from there."*

Make space in the classroom for spontaneous creativity to bloom. You always want to have something up your sleeve—a teacher should never be caught unawares when it comes to teaching material—but know that you don't always have to use it at the time, or in the order, you intended. Strictly adhering to a lesson plan simply because it's part of your "plan" can result in a progressively stale learning environment and missed opportunities of all sorts.

Don't be afraid to walk in with a loose plan and intend to read and respond to your students' moods. Like Justin, you might just pull out a guitar and collectively birth a new project everyone is invested in. Be sensitive to those hunches in your gut about where your students and class time may be leading. Don't be afraid to riff on an established lesson plan or change course if, in the moment, things feel stuck. Be prepared, but trust your instincts as a professional and follow the lead of your students. Do they seem excited about a certain idea or activity? Follow that! Channel their excitement and incorporate their interests into the objectives you have on deck. Consider project-based learning, personalized assignments, student-directed activities, and other creative ways to learn in the classroom. Improvise and experiment. Respond and pivot.

How can you create flexible space for you and your kids to shape a lesson's direction in real time? How can you practice following your intuition on the fly?

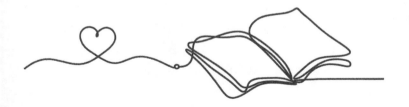

# Kelli Wilson

*Tulsa, Oklahoma*

## Moment of Impact

This is a story about Mark.

We all knew a Mark in school. He's the kid who rarely spoke, sat in the back of the class, wore black from head to toe, and walked with his shoulder rubbing against the wall of an uncrowded hallway. Everyone was aware of Mark, but few of us—if any—really knew him. We didn't know about the violent storm raging inside him because his quiet exterior hid it from view and dampened its fury.

As assistant principal, I had heard about Mark through my conversations with teachers. He appeared on my radar early as a student who needed something. What he needed I couldn't know, but experience told me he needed my attention, whether he wanted it or not. Each day offered me a new opportunity to invest a few minutes of my time into Mark's life. These investments came in the form of conversations at lunch, in the hallway between classes, or after school while he waited for the bus. It was a struggle at times to find things to talk about. Mark wasn't what you would call an open book and he would likely have preferred I leave him alone, which is what everyone else did.

As time passed, though, our conversations became less one sided. There were even moments he would approach me. One day, toward the end of the school year and nearly two years after I first talked to him, Mark walked into my office and plopped himself down into one of the chairs across from my desk.

It had been one of those days for Mark. A day when the darkness within him began to permeate his reality. When he looked around him at everything and everyone, he saw them through an ever-darkening haze. He spoke in low, labored tones, as if the weight of his existence were laying ominously across his chest, challenging his every breath and hope for normalcy. My heart broke for him as he lamented. I saw myself in him: just a lonely kid with circumstances far beyond what he should be expected to handle.

When Mark grew quiet, I began to fill the silence. My words were well meant, but as I spoke them, they seemed to lift and dissipate like vapor. The moment was proving to be far too heavy for words of any kind. As if to prove this, Mark slowly began digging into his pocket. He found his car keys and pulled them into view. As I kept trying to penetrate the fog around him with encouragement and positivity, Mark grabbed one of the keys with his right hand. Placing the jagged edge of the key to his left wrist, he deliberately and without pause drew the key up his wrist, tearing his skin and the soft tissue beneath. Mark's blood began to spray from his body, but he didn't let up. He was emotionless.

As I leaped across my desk, I had only one thought: *You cannot let anything happen to him.* My hands met his wound, covering it with a panicked grip. Hearing my screams, the office staff came running, and in time so did the nurse. Mark was ushered away from me by paramedics that day, and after that incident, he was kept away from school by the demands and recommendations of mental-health professionals and protocols.

As often happens in education, I moved to another position in another district at the end of that school year. I thought of Mark often, but I only saw him in my memory. He remained frozen in time, the same small and quiet tenth grader I had known.

Years later, on a cold Friday night, I stood in front of the student section at our school's football stadium. My gaze fixed on the crowd, I was startled by two large hands as they covered my eyes from behind. A deep, gravelly voice exclaimed, "Ms. Wilson, you're not gonna believe this!" Those hands spun me around to reveal Mark. But it wasn't the Mark of my memory—it was a grown man with broad shoulders, a towering frame, and a full, bright smile. I stood speechless, struck by the shock of having him in front of me, real after all those years. Mark's presence was commanding and confident as he said, "Ms. Wilson, I wouldn't be here if it wasn't for you. You saved my life every day when I was in ninth and tenth grade."

Again, Mark and I were in a situation that was too significant for words. In that moment, I embraced him once again, not in terror or sadness but in love. The relief and joy of seeing him once again, healthy and well, manifested in tears.

Our conversation allowed me to piece together his journey from that day when he was a tenth grader in my office to now. He described how he obtained the mental-health support he so desperately needed. He talked about how he graduated from high school, how he was employed and working towards his college degree. I sensed and saw a lightness, an ease, about Mark as we talked. I was profoundly happy for him and so grateful that he was well and whole. That he was still here.

At last, with the help of his mother and others, Mark had found his way out of the darkness.

## Path into Education

Why teaching? Of all the options available, what compelled me to become a teacher? Growing up, school was my lifeline. I wanted to be that lifeline, that refuge, for others.

As a child, school was an escape from the unpredictability of my home life. When I was eight years old, my parents divorced, and my mom moved my siblings and me to California. At the time, Mom was showing behavior consistent with bipolar disorder. She was using drugs to self-medicate, among other dubious activities, and her distress had an unmooring effect on us. We inherited her trauma. She loved us but didn't know how to parent us.

Those were lost years, chaotic years that made no sense, years that stood in the place of what a childhood should be.

Every morning, I woke my sisters and brother and got us out the door for school, our singular safe haven. Mom was absent, if not physically then emotionally. Eventually, she sent the four of us back to Oklahoma from California. On a Greyhound bus. Alone.

As the oldest, it was my job to stay alert during the bus ride, waking my siblings at the rest stops, making sure we were eating enough. I had to ensure we made it safely home, or at least to the next place we were going to live. It didn't feel like "home" existed.

Once we arrived in Oklahoma, Dad was there, but he relinquished custody to the state. He wanted us to be in a household full of love and stability, which was more than he thought he could give to us. My siblings and I lived for a while in a temporary shelter, but ultimately, we were placed in the foster-care system. In separate homes.

I still remember those bittersweet Sundays. Dad would pick up the four of us to spend a few hours together. That time was precious—the part of the week we each craved most. At the end of the day, when Dad began dropping off each sibling at their respective foster home, we would all cry. The crying continued until the last one of us was dropped off. Alone.

Ultimately, in 1973, all four of us moved into the same cottage at the Baptist Children's Home where we remained until we all graduated from high school. Amid the tumult of moving from place to place, home to home, being wrenched away from my siblings, one parent and then another, the one thing that had been constant in my life was school.

At school, there was routine. I saw the same faces at the same times every day. While most students find this monotony unbearable, it was solace to me. I was comforted in knowing there was security and constancy to my school days.

As an adult, I wanted to return to the school setting and be part of creating that sanctuary for someone else. Someone like Mark. Everyone brings unspoken stories into the building, and most of the time, we have no idea what kinds of battles are being fought at home. At school, I had teachers like Peggy McGehee who believed in me. I had coaches that motivated, guided, and supported me. So much of my childhood, I felt alone, struggling to do the right thing without any real guidance. School and my teachers provided community—one I desperately longed for.

Finally, I had found adults who loved me and could care for me the way I really needed. I had found a place where I didn't have to be the most responsible person in the room. I didn't need to have a plan or prepare for the worst-case scenario or wonder what kind of trouble I might be walking into.

I benefited so deeply from my teachers and coaches, and I'm grateful for the opportunity to pour myself into students' lives the way those amazing educators poured into me. I am a teacher because I love students. I want to empower and support them. I want to give them a place to belong. A safe haven. A refuge. A home.

## Best Practice

*"He had appeared on my radar early on as a student who needed something. What he needed I couldn't know,*

*but experience told me he needed my attention, whether he wanted it or not."*

Every school day presents a new opportunity to love, serve, and educate students. Identify those students you know need something from you, something beyond a solid lesson plan or some extra help after school. Sometimes, what a student needs is something you're not equipped to give, but there is always a way to show them you care. Make an effort to give them your attention daily. This could be through a conversation, a simple greeting each morning, an encouraging word after class when it seems they've had a hard day, or even just a smile. Be aware of your students and their emotional health as best as you can be. Small gestures often speak far louder than we know.

Is there a student who needs regular acknowledgement and affirmation from you? How can you provide that in a healthy, sustainable way?

# Rachel Whalen

*Montpelier, Vermont*

## Moment of Impact

Those who can't do, teach.

This idea is pervasive in American culture, and unfortunately, it has seeped into not only the public's perception of educators but also the beliefs of educators themselves. This sentiment destabilizes our professional confidence and, in some cases, prevents it from developing altogether. In a chronically undervalued field like education, it can be almost impossible to look back on your career—no matter how far along the road you are—and feel true satisfaction in what you've accomplished. It's hard to silence the nagging voices that accuse you of not being good enough or say that no matter what you've done, it's never enough.

Despite this resistance, I noticed a new comfort in my career once I had been at my school site for ten years. I knew my way around the building, was established with my colleagues, and had a positive reputation among the students. I felt like I was finally in a position where I had enough clout to advocate for my students and teammates and really influence change. I was asking fewer questions and I had more answers.

Then a new principal came to my school.

That's one thing about education that guarantees you stay engaged and never feel you've completed the race: change is never-ending and everywhere, every hour. Classes rotate, students come in and out, and faculty and staffing changes alter the dynamics within the building. But I don't mind. Education's fluid nature keeps me on my toes and reminds me to stay sharp. I enjoy researching new instructional methods, introducing new activities, and implementing new strategies to facilitate student understanding. However, navigating dynamics with new staff members is a bit more complicated. New administrators are always a wild card. The role of principal is especially one that can have immeasurable impact on your experience.

Fortunately, I met Mr. Richards and immediately felt seen and valued. He was interested in my self-perception and my growth and development as a professional. In my experience, these areas were ones I alone was concerned with. Certainly, my principal hadn't truly cared about them on my behalf before. Yet here was Mr. Richards, asking me pointed questions, encouraging me to step more fully into self-confidence, and protecting me and my time in the classroom.

In one of our initial conversations, we talked at length about the distinction I perceived between being a "teacher" and being an "educator." To me, the former is a position to be filled, a body occupying space. Someone who does the job of teaching students. An educator, on the other hand, is a professional, one whose influence can't be quantified, and an individual whose expertise is respected and prized. This is a person who changes the lives of students and edifies the people and places around her.

"Why don't you see yourself as an educator?" Mr. Richards asked me.

I didn't have a proper answer. I was well-established in my career by that point, was serving on meaningful committees in my building, and had formed strong relationships with my colleagues and kids. Yet I didn't see myself as an educator. I could see the other educators on my team and at my site that way, but when it came to looking at myself objectively, there was a block I couldn't overcome.

Over the course of our time together, Mr. Richards continued to affirm me. At every turn, he reminded me who I really was and who I still am: an educator. He passed along professional-development opportunities he thought would interest and serve his faculty well. He validated my work and the work of every member of his faculty. He saw our profession as a real profession!

Having Mr. Richards as my principal was a turning point for me. Even though I had been an educator for over a decade, our working relationship was the first one in which I felt like a true partner with my administration. And it wasn't just that Mr. Richards saw me as a colleague. I could see myself as his colleague as well. His arrival at my school site was the impetus for greater self-reflection.

Though I didn't have a response to his question at the time, in the years since, I have been on an ongoing quest to answer it. I've taken it upon myself to carve out my identity as an educator, to fortify my self-esteem, and to deepen the respect and admiration I feel for my own expertise and skills. I try to view my own accomplishments and achievements the way I would those of my teammates. I strive to celebrate and champion myself the way I aspire to celebrate and champion my friends.

While Mr. Richards and I no longer work together, the value he saw in me and helped me see in myself is a gift I have taken with me. Students and colleagues come in and out of classrooms and buildings, but the things we learn from them and the memories made with them last. I've learned things from colleagues and administrators that have critically formed me as an educator and shaped my philosophy and approach. I've observed techniques, ideas, and projects of brilliant educators. I've attended workshops and trainings and gained new ways to communicate familiar concepts. But the most important revelations have been gradual developments, the values and principles I must be steeped in over time. The questions posed by others I could neither answer nor shake and have wrestled with for years.

Sometimes, there are clear turning points in a story where you know exactly when you have moved from one place to the next. Other times, progress is slower and sneaks up on you unexpectedly, a change you don't discern until suddenly you look up and are surprised to find you've arrived. I'll never reach the point of teaching mastery where I have nothing else to learn or no other way to grow, but the journey is most significant anyway. By carrying all the lessons I've learned over the years with me, from colleagues and students and parents and administrators, I am never emptyhanded and am always ready to face what comes. With these gifts, I remember that I am an educator. I always have been.

## Path into Education

The structured world of academia has always made sense to me. The schedule was reliable, steadfast as clockwork. I knew the faces that would surround me and when. When it came to schoolwork, I understood clearly the equations bound up in education. For me, the input of high effort was likely to yield an output of success. More organizations meant more people, which produced more friendships and a deeper investment in my own learning. These kinds of certainties didn't oppress or restrict me. I liked them and their solid predictability. In fact, I loved school. It was in my blood.

Growing up, my mother was a fixture in the world of education. A speech pathologist, she contracted to come into schools and work with preschool students, and I have fond memories of tagging along as she worked. Sometimes, when childcare got bungled, my brother and I went with her on her school visits, but I loved those days. In the summer, when I was off from school, I begged my mom to take me with her when she worked summer school. I ate up the learning environment. The rhythms of school were natural to me, yet the unknown of what they would present each day kept me riveted.

School is a place of performance. Students prepare and rehearse their material and must recall it with precision, producing it on demand in a variety of forms. In education, we've come a long way in terms of grasping the importance of learning styles, malleable intelligence, and scaffolding to better serve students and tailor lessons and methods to their distinct learning approaches. But no matter how I was tested on my knowledge, I thrived on the rush of performance. I was very achievement oriented, and quizzes, flashcards, and essay outlines were my comforting familiars. As I entered high school, I developed a passion for writing, and that found its main outlet in my history class. Document-based questions became quick ways to my heart, and I frequently had conversations with my teacher, Mr. Swanson, about assignments, historical movements, and life. After school, I'd meander toward his classroom. One day, he said something that has stayed with me all these years later.

"Have you ever noticed, Rachel, that you always end up at the podium?"

I hadn't. He nodded, a knowing smile on his face.

"You're going to be a teacher one day."

But I wasn't. I loved writing and language and decided to study journalism and communications as an undergraduate. Education was my mom's thing; it was something I was good at and enjoyed, but it wasn't my future.

My nearest brush with teaching during college was an after-school tutoring program I participated in. I volunteered with fifth and sixth graders and had a great time. They were funny and lively, and it was rewarding to see them work through tough material and reap the fruit of their hard work and focus—one of those faithful equations of school I was such a fan of.

Turns out, I couldn't get enough of the students I was supporting or the success they were realizing for themselves. I began to gravitate toward the tutoring building, arriving on days even when I wasn't scheduled to be there. This started happening more and more, a habit I seemed to have developed unconsciously, much like the one I created with Mr. Swanson's podium. Eventually, I opened my eyes fully. I realized I didn't have to compartmentalize this feeling or this experience. I could champion students and their learning for the rest of my life. I could be a teacher.

So I changed my major and shifted to what seems now like an inevitable fit: early-childhood education. Another something I must have picked up without knowing it—following the path my mom's footsteps had beaten before me. When I went back to visit Mr. Swanson and tell him I'd made the switch to education, he beamed. He had known it before I did and was proud of me. That affirmation was powerful, and I felt my confidence bolstered by his support. He had seen me when I was a student, really seen me, and not only had he been right, but he also gave me a glimpse of the influence I could have with my own students in the future.

As an educator, I am where I'm meant to be. I love school and I love my kids, but the dearest refuges I have while in the trenches are my coworkers. There is a core group of women, fellow educators, who keep me grounded, who keep me joyful, and who keep me present. Work wives. We see each other through the day-to-day struggles and celebrate one another's big triumphs and small victories. It is an inexpressible balm to have people I trust and treasure, who do the same work I do, to bounce ideas off of, to sympathize with me, and to fortify my spirits and strength.

Education—any occupation or endeavor for that matter—is what you make it. You will get out of it what you put into it, and these relationships with my colleagues are part of the delight and fun I experience. They help me remember my potential and worth as an educator and remind me I am more than "just a teacher." There is always more to learn and know and be challenged by in this profession, and though I am teaching others, I am still a student. Every day offers a new lesson to learn, a new opportunity to seize, and new possibilities to explore and realize.

It is thrilling to have a front-row seat to my students' learning. I have the behind-the-scenes privilege of witnessing the hard work they put into learning something new, yet I also have the joy of watching their confidence bloom, their skills improve, and their fascination and curiosity with ideas spark. To see them grow, to hear them laugh, to help shape them for their future—these are delights so priceless and dear to me, I will keep coming back for them day after day after day after day.

## Best Practice

*"It is thrilling to have a front-row seat to my students' learning. [...] To see them grow, to hear them laugh, to help shape them for their future—these are delights so priceless and dear to me, I will keep coming back for them day after day after day after day."*

The most important part of education is the relationship with your students. Everything else is bonus. It's important to know what you're doing, and it's nice to have a beautiful classroom. It makes a difference when you work well with your team and communicate regularly with parents. You can have immaculate storage cabinets and the most perfectly timed lesson plans. But the cornerstone of success is the student relationship. What your kids really want is a genuine connection with you and to know and see who you truly are. You are, and can be, enough for them.

Take the pulse of your student relationships. Evaluate where you can work a bit harder to get to know particular students, then go out of your way this week to reach out to them. Reflect on your lesson plans and unit structures. Are there lessons with too many bells and whistles that could be simplified to prioritize student connection? What kind of difference does that make in your classroom?

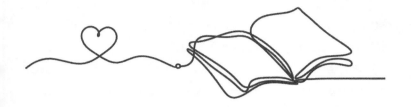

# Monte Syrie

*Cheney, Washington*

## Moment of Impact

Connection and community. You cannot have one without the other.

Without these two aspects of life, people are lost. We were made for relationship with one another. Not cursory, surface-level relationship—real, intimate, messy relationship. This is a need everybody feels, whether they acknowledge it or not. Building strong, genuine connections with my students and providing a safe place for them to do the same with one another are my highest priorities in the classroom. Plus, kids can smell fake from a mile away, so living out this authenticity as a teacher is absolutely crucial.

So, how do I work to make connections with kids and provide them with opportunities to connect with each other?

For twelve years, I had done an activity in my monthly department meetings with my fellow teachers: Smiles and Frowns. Some people call this Highs and Lows, others call it Roses and Thorns. Regardless of moniker, it's the idea that every person has a chance to share something positive going on in their life and something not so positive. My colleagues and I benefitted from this practice and enjoyed it quite a bit, so I thought I'd give it a try with my students.

Regularly, I begin class with this activity, yielding the floor to students so they can share their Smiles and Frowns. Perhaps even more importantly, I give them the power to pass if they don't want to say anything. I am much more interested in their commitment than their compliance, and even students who choose not to speak up benefit. They value hearing from their peers and sharing life together in this small but intentional way.

Doing this activity in my classes has made a huge difference to my students and to me. But why? Why does intentionally connecting with students every day matter?

Shouldn't content take precedence in the classroom? What about all that lost instructional time? To answer these questions, I'd like to share a personal experience. Then you can judge for yourself.

As usual, my class began the hour by going through our Smiles and Frowns. On this particular day, students were sharing their aspirations—dream jobs, hopes for the future. It was Rebecca's turn to respond, and she said she wanted to be a teacher. I was dumbfounded on so many levels and for so many reasons. This admission came straight out of left field, and I hadn't had any inkling it was coming.

As someone who prides himself on knowing his students and taking a genuine interest in them—really *knowing* their desires, their passions, their motivators—I was stunned to hear this revelation. How could I value closeness with my students if I hadn't known an essential detail like this, especially one that was so close to my own heart?

Learning that one of my students wanted to become a teacher and knowing I had wasted so much time when I could've been shaping and guiding her in her pursuit of that path was a failure. As a teacher, you are a steward of your students' time, gifts, and potential. It is within your power to help mold young people and support them as they find their voice. I knew those days, those moments of opportunity, were squandered.

I could never meet Rebecca at just those times and in just those ways ever again.

Part of why Rebecca's goal shocked me so greatly was because she hadn't struck me as an individual filled with great ambition. I saw her every day and ascribed to her certain beliefs, perceptions, and assumptions. I viewed her as a stereotype instead of a dynamic person with unique dreams and the potential for self-realization. My mistreatment of her knocks the wind out of me still and fills me with shame.

Had I known Rebecca wanted to be a teacher, I would have altered my entire approach toward her. It's like professing you want to be a surgeon in front of the surgeon you've been working alongside for months. Think of all the times they could've apprenticed you in the operating room. The tips and tricks they could've shared with you that they learned the hard way on their journey. The encouragement and support they could've lent you as you began to follow in their footsteps.

I've since lost contact with Rebecca, and wondering where she is now keeps me up at night. Not knowing how her life could have been different if I had gotten out of my own way and seen her with a clear gaze. No biases. No preconceived notions. I don't mean to exaggerate my potential impact on her life, but I lament losing my chance to help. How could I have supported her along the way to being a teacher? I may never know. And it's this mystery of education, and teaching specifically, that I no longer take for granted.

I don't even *entertain* the possibility of not knowing my students. I do not tolerate relational ambiguity. I want to know and understand and appreciate students, and I want to give them opportunities to cultivate that depth with me and with their classmates.

Connection is the foundation of trust. With it, there's no guarantee you'll earn someone's trust, but without it, you have no hope of doing so. It's not a triviality. It is essential. It is the crux of what we do in education, the precursor to everything we hope to accomplish in a semester or a year with our students. When you teach a subject to your students, you're asking them to trust you. Not only that, but you're asking them to trust you enough to buy into your content and believe it will come in handy somehow in the future. There has to be a starting point for that trust. There must be a place where it can grow and strengthen over time.

That place is the classroom, and the way it happens is through building relationships.

My kids may not remember the things I taught them, but they will never forget the way I made them feel. My hope is that, by taking the time every day to pause and give them the choice to speak or stay silent, each of them understands that they are the most important thing in the room to me.

## Path into Education

My childhood was a time of lean living. My family and I scrounged and scraped to get by. We had very little, and what we did have was usually broken or misshapen, never new. I was a product of two divorces, so the idea of constancy and having something to keep, something that was really and truly mine, was as unfamiliar and remote to me as anything possibly could be.

But then there was school. Things at school were whole.

An absent student was noticed by teachers. Routines existed and expectations were upheld. You could trust that the bell was going to ring at 9:45 every morning. People and practices were reliable and could be depended upon. But most importantly, it was apparent to me that a class was much more than the sum of its parts.

At school, things made sense. Every hour, I had a place to belong. There was a group of people looking for me and I could contribute to our time in a meaningful way. Each classroom was full of promise. I received the lessons my teachers prepared expectantly. These were my opportunities to grab. And no teacher gave me such rich opportunities like Mr. Hamrick.

I was an eighth grader in the 1980s. Mr. Hamrick was my English Language Arts teacher, and while I found refuge inside the school building, life outside it was confusing and frightening. The AIDS epidemic was rampant and pervasive, and the uncertainty everyone felt was unparalleled at the time, though things have changed in that regard now in light of the pandemic and other concerns. As with many complex topics, most adults wouldn't speak plainly about AIDS, but Mr. Hamrick would.

Some friends and I approached him with our burning questions, and I remember he spoke to us like we were adults. He didn't give us more information than we needed. He didn't divulge inappropriate details. But he told us the truth. He leveled with us and cut through the flood of misinformation. He legitimized our fears and, in turn, us. By simply answering our questions and speaking the facts, he communicated to us that, yeah, we deserved to know what was going on. We had rights and dignity and curiosities the same as adults. He empowered us to consider our own thoughts and values. Not as subordinates, but as fellow human beings. This one conversation changed everything for me.

And that's the magic of education: a student's life can pivot on a single moment, the trajectory of their future hinging upon one relationship.

Because of Mr. Hamrick, I became a first-generation college student. Because of his class, I became an English Language Arts teacher. Because he cared enough to tell the truth and challenge us students to embrace our worth, I became an educator who understands the power of personal connection.

Education has the power to connect kids. Classrooms throw together a mix of students that will likely never reunite of their own volition. This setting gives them the chance to grow in empathy, emotional intelligence, and tolerance. You can't put a price on that. As a student, that's the kind of world I wanted to live in, the kind of world Mr. Hamrick made me yearn for and believe was possible. As an adult, it's still the kind of world I want and one I believe in so hard, I wake up every day and go to bat for it.

While students' time in our classrooms is temporary, you can still build things with them that last. You do this by the way you accept them. In that moment when they were down and you made them laugh, gave them space, or let them simply sit in silence beside you. Think back to your own time as a student. I do. The memories I made at school and the ways my teachers made me feel, the gifts of kindness and respect and self-confidence—those were things I could keep. I want to give my kids things they can keep, too.

## Best Practice

*"I realized [Smiles and Frowns] is powerful, not just in terms of me getting to know my kids, but the thing I didn't expect that happened was how well they got to know each other. Another consequence I didn't foresee was the capacity for it to develop empathy among them. So it's*

*not just about knowing my neighbor. It's about under-standing my neighbor and feeling empathy for them, cheering their successes and supporting them through their hardships."*

Creating safety and community in the classroom is paramount. Learning and growth are built on a foundation of security, and you should prioritize that emotional security in the classroom. Make time at the beginning of class for students to contribute to and develop that environment and implement activities daily in which you *all* can get to know each other. This example activity from Monte was so effective when used in groups of faculty members that he brought it to his classroom.

Roses and Thorns, Highs and Lows, Smiles and Frowns. It is known by many names, but the spirit is the same. In this activity, invite students to share a positive moment from their day, week, or weekend with the class. This is the rose/high/smile, etc. Then invite them to also share a moment that may have disappointed or bothered them. This is the thorn/low/frown, etc. Empower students with the ability to pass if they want to. Some of Monte's students chose to abstain from the activity in class, but they still enjoyed hearing their classmates' contributions. As the teacher, you should also participate. It's important to lead by example when establishing trust with students. Don't ask them to do something you're unwilling to do.

Try this in your classes at least once in the next two weeks. See what kind of difference it makes in your relationships with students and their rapport among themselves. Remember that you're in control of this activity. Keep it on track and protect the voices of your students from any rogue detractors.

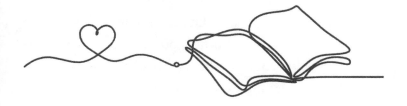

# Pam Swan

*Greensboro, North Carolina*

## Moment of Impact

I met Emily when she completed first grade for the first time. When she was meant to enter second grade, she could barely read, and her phonics skills were far below where they should have been. As her second-grade teacher, I recognized there were gaps in her learning that the second-grade curriculum likely wouldn't fill; on the contrary, it would probably overwhelm and frustrate her, rendering school an emblem of defeat and futility. I voiced my concerns, and after a few conferences and some assessments, I recommended that Emily repeat first grade. While it's no one's first choice to be "held back"—and a task no educator takes pleasure in—I believed it was the right decision, and one that would end up serving Emily well in the long run.

There were a lot of contributing factors as to why she was behind at the time. Though she was only five years old, her home life had already undergone massive upheaval, and the extra year would give her the room and stability to strengthen her literacy, develop more maturity, and grow even more excited to progress to the next grade.

I remember passing her in the hallways during her repeat year. She would skip up to me, beaming like she had a secret, and say, "Mrs. Swan, I'm gonna get you next year!"

By the time Emily was one of my second-grade students, she was more than ready, and I'd developed an extra degree of tenderness in my heart toward her. As I got to know her better, I learned more about her family and what life was like for her when she left at the end of the school day. I discovered that Emily had no mother at home; her mom had died when she was six weeks old. Her father was battling an illness that prevented him from being the consistent, healthy parent he wanted to be and that Emily needed him to be. Plus, he had two other young girls—Emily's sisters—he was trying to raise at the same time. The more I got to know this precious little girl who worked so hard to reach my second-grade class and who worked even harder at home, the softer my heart became toward her. She needed to be anchored by something. Or someone. So I volunteered.

As her teacher, it was my responsibility to educate her with important concepts, to help her learn the building blocks of language, math, science, and social studies so she would be prepared for what was to come in the future.

But also, as her teacher, it was my privilege and honor to be by her side and offer my care, time, and attention during a very difficult period of her life.

As the school year wore on, Emily and I began spending more and more time together. We created a fun routine of going for ice cream once a week. We would talk about anything that popped into our heads: the plots of our favorite T.V. shows, the big and small worries that sometimes kept us up at night, why singing along to the radio in our pajamas was so fun, where we hoped to be in ten years. We developed a rare bond composed of two equally precious halves—one was that of a classroom teacher with a beloved student and the other was more akin to that of a mother with her daughter. Sometimes, when she would arrive at school out of sorts, I would give her a hug and tenderly brush her hair before the day began, smoothing her flyaways and her worried nerves. Our families even celebrated Thanksgiving together.

It was never my intention to stand in for Emily's mother. No one could do that. But it was my intention to show her she was loved and cherished. I did my best to take care of her and look out for her as much as was appropriate. I wanted her to know she was special. I saw a student in need who, regardless of her challenges at home, still needed to learn. I did what I could to meet her needs educationally, physically, and emotionally.

Ours was, and remains, a once-in-a-lifetime bond.

Emily is in her twenties now, and we text regularly. It has been a joy to watch her grow and become a strong, flourishing woman. As her father has recovered from his illness, her relationship with him has healed as well, and knowing she now enjoys him in a complete, abundant way delights me to no end. I want what's best for her, and seeing how she has worked toward and obtained the life and relationships she desires for herself … well, there's nothing more my heart could ask for.

What makes this relationship even more distinct is that it is a continuation of another memorable relationship. I saw firsthand the life-altering power of an educator who treasures her students through my fifth-grade teacher, Mrs. Payne. It's astounding the impact one adult can have on a child, for better or worse. Mrs. Payne made me feel like I was one of a kind, like I was somebody who had a lot to offer in the world. She helped me realize that even though I came from a family where education was a low priority, and for some of my family members an impossibility, I was smart and could achieve the things I wanted. I saw that story repeating itself in a new way with Emily.

Even though she repeated first grade. Even though her dad struggled with his own issues. Even though she lost her mom and had no memory of her. *Even though.* Education and learning were there to help her move forward and get ready for the rest of her life, whatever she wanted it to be.

I wanted Emily to know her background didn't define her. The beginnings of our stories needn't determine the endings. While there are circumstances and obstacles that prevent us all from starting at the same place, there are also opportunities and individuals along the way who can help us make progress and change course.

I was able to be one of those people for Emily because Mrs. Payne had been one of those people for me.

## Path into Education

I was in the fifth grade the first time I was treated like a real person instead of just a little kid.

My teacher, Mrs. Payne, was in the first year of her career. She was young and vibrant, full of energy and still possessed of the optimism and joy that all too often fades over a long tenure in the classroom. She was beautiful and fun and brightened each room she entered. She was a living sunbeam and lit up every bit of my class-mates and me, from our toes to our curious minds.

Elementary school was a hard time for me. My parents were divorced, and I had some health issues that disrupted my schooling and kept me in and out of the hospital. I entered fifth grade pretty far behind. My reading level was low, and I exhibited signs of dyslexia, though it was the 1960s and no one yet knew anything about that. I felt hopeless and helpless to get caught up. I was Eeyore, shadowed by my own little rain cloud of self-doubt and insecurity wherever I went. Until Mrs. Payne walked into my life and cleared the sky.

In so many ways, Mrs. Payne was ahead of her time. Research on malleable intelligence and emotional intelligence was virtually nonexistent. But there was a fire in Mrs. Payne that burned so brightly and emanated such warmth to her students, we experienced the benefits of that thinking anyway. She established relational connections with each of us. She saw us as grownups-in-training, celebrated the distinct traits we had, treated us with dignity, and entrusted us with responsibility. She homed in on our unique skills and praised them in front of our classmates.

"Louis, why don't you come up here to the board and draw this out for the class? Everyone, let's watch Louis draw this picture. Isn't he such a great artist?"

I didn't feel like a strong student, and it was hard for me to see my positive qualities, but I felt valued by Mrs. Payne. She let me set up the craft tables and lay out supplies, run errands to the office, and pass out worksheets to my classmates. Her trust in me built up my confidence and gave me strength. Reflecting on Mrs. Payne's encouragements prompted a shift in my spirit and instilled a sense of pride in myself and my work I hadn't had before. Slowly, I began to make up the ground I had lost due to my periods of being home sick instead of in school. Through our relationship, Mrs. Payne transformed my outlook on education and restored my dismal self-esteem.

Her kindness didn't just change me, though; she transformed my class of dissimilar students into a united family. She was hands on with us, leading us in activities where we could play and learn alongside one another, and she was patient when we didn't understand things.

"It's okay, Pam. Let's do it again." We would try once more. "That's great! Want to do it one more time to make sure it sticks?"

She didn't rush us and met us right where we were. She asked for our opinions and valued what we thought, even as ten-year-olds. By letting her guard down, she modeled honesty and humility for us, and these behaviors directly translated into us mastering objectives, building a classroom community, and having fun. I remember on the last day of school, we capped off our time together as a class by sitting on top of our desks and talking about our favorite moments from the year. And when Mrs. Payne got married that June, we were all invited to the wedding.

After I left the fifth grade, I knew I wanted to grow up and be just like her. And that's what I did.

All through junior high and high school, I set myself on the track to be an educator, and I never wavered from it. I became a second-grade teacher and aspired to follow Mrs. Payne's example and make my students feel the way she made me feel. Part of what drew me to second grade was the powerful reading foundation laid that year. As a struggling reader once, I am now a huge reading advocate for my students. I try to help them see reading as an important building block of their future, and I often tell students, "If you can learn to read, you can read to learn. Whatever you want! Anything you're interested in. You can read and learn all about those areas for the rest of your life. But reading comes first."

I want my students to feel powerful, confident, and important. Elementary school is a critical time for creating lifelong learners, and my aim is to encourage students and fill them up whenever I can. I remember Mrs. Payne's light and strive to bring my own into the classroom, shining it onto those students caught in the shadow of their personal battles. I work hard to foster safety and love in our classroom culture, so we don't have to shy away from hard concepts or discomfort. We can move toward a challenge, figure out something new, and finish it off with a laugh and a smile.

It's no overstatement to say Mrs. Payne changed my life. Her class was the exemplar for me, the template I used when trying to create a wonderful student experience and when trying to emulate a master teacher's classroom practices. Creativity, collaboration, and our common humanity are the principles that guided me in my career. I'm retired now, but those are ideals I first learned in Mrs. Payne's fifth-grade classroom. Not a day goes by that I don't think of her or feel gratitude for that formative experience. In fact, rarely does a week go by that I don't speak to her on the phone. Now both in our late 60s and 70s, we've seen a lot of life and have spent decades in the classroom, and we both look back with fondness on the school year that brought us together. It changed both our lives in indelible ways.

While Mrs. Payne viewed our time through the lens of work, and I saw our class time as bursts of fun, what we were really doing was building a bond. Time-tested and proven, that bond remains unbroken.

## Best Practice

*"She didn't rush us and met us right where we were. She asked for our opinions and valued what we thought, even as ten-year-olds."*

Humility in the classroom goes further than we know. Even though there is a clear division between who the authority figure is (you) and who should defer to that leadership (your students), leading from a place of humility and compassion distinguishes good educators from great ones. Like Pam's fifth-grade teacher, Mrs. Payne, meeting students with gentleness and patiently inviting their voices into dialogue with yours can reinforce learning academic standards, help students become more assertive and independent, and validate them for who they are. When Pam revealed her own vulnerabilities to students— like admitting she, too, was nervous on the first day of school—she saw that this act built trust and immediately closed the distance between her and her students.

Look for opportunities to humble yourself before your students, even if it's uncomfortable or scary. How can you introduce a regular practice of vulnerability in front of your classes? Where can you relinquish control and position students to lead and be keepers of the culture?

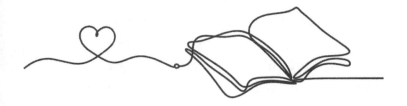

# Tonya Bobo
*North Little Rock, Arkansas*

## Moment of Impact

There are times in life that make us who we are. Those moments when you're not sure if you can make it through, but somehow you do, and that survival changes you. In spite of all the odds, you fought the good fight and came out on top.

Except sometimes, you don't come out on top. At least not in the way you expected.

One of these moments came after I had been teaching at my school site for five years. This place and I had a long, rich history. It was where I first realized my love for education. I subbed for the very first time at this school and had my first bona fide teaching gig here. It was where my children attended. I knew countless students, teachers, and families. It was my community. It was special to me. I didn't want to be anywhere else.

You can guess what comes next, can't you?

As a kindergarten teacher, it is my honor to teach students how to read. We work through the letters of the alphabet, the sounds those letters make when they're by themselves and when they're grouped together. We firm up the shaky ground some students are standing on in the fall, and they emerge more solid and confident come spring.

I'm passionate about this age group and this critical skill, and to deepen my expertise, I'd participated in some intensive educator training. In addition, I was a member of the Arkansas Teacher Corps, an organization committed to helping teachers provide equitable educational experiences, so I was receiving not only instructional best practices and classroom tactics from my professional development; I was also being strengthened as an educator and encouraged to advocate for myself and my students, however that might look in my daily role. I entered the school year poised for success and ready to put my new tools into action.

This particular year, the administration wanted to roll out a new approach to phonics instruction across the grade level. However, it became clear pretty quickly that the proposed curriculum and methods would not facilitate my students' learning. I knew my kids. I knew what worked for them and what didn't. This was *my* school, the community I belonged to and loved, and I just knew this wasn't the best fit for my kiddos. It was going to confuse them, frustrate them, and leave them defeated, the complete opposite conditions I want for my students.

Emboldened by the support of the Teacher Corps and affirmed in my instructional instincts through my recent PD workshops, I took my concerns to the administration, but they didn't listen. They brushed me off and didn't heed any of my warnings. It felt like their tunnel vision and singular focus on this new rollout disallowed any sort of opposition. Their attitudes brooked no disagreement, no difference of opinion, and ultimately no humility. This communicated myriad upsetting and disheartening messages, not the least of which was that they didn't trust me to be a professional. They didn't give me the freedom to go do what I do well.

I couldn't in good conscience present something to my students I was certain would confound them. So I decided to tweak the provided curriculum. We focused on the same objectives, hit the same benchmarks, and accomplished the same end goals—My kids could sound out words. They could write. They could read!—but we went about it a little differently than prescribed.

This was not a secret I kept from the administration. In fact, it wasn't a secret I could've kept even if I wanted to. I had observers in my classroom constantly. You know how information spreads in schools. Something is hinted at in passing or spoken under a person's breath, and then suddenly, it's everywhere all at once. But I wasn't afraid. I knew my approach was right for my students, and my students are always my top concern. Doing what is best for them is what I must do. Period.

Unfortunately, my administration didn't see it this way. Around the middle of the year, I was notified that my contract would not be renewed at the year's end. This was a blow, but as an educator, it's an occupational hazard. Pink slips. Layoffs. Nonexistent funding. Depleted resources. I was disappointed, but I persevered in giving my students what they needed. The real teaching and the real learning are what I'm interested in. Not playing politics and appeasing administrators who have never taught at the grade level they're aiming to influence and who contradict even one another in what the best course of action should be. I continued serving my students the best way I knew how, and I kept working closely with the other kindergarten teacher. She was fairly new, so I had been sharing my lesson plans and activities with her throughout the year. We were doing more or less the same things in both of our classrooms, but you know what's interesting? One of us had a contract renewal offer, and one of us didn't.

In mid-March, the administration brought in literacy experts to evaluate the school's instructional methods and conduct classroom observations. When they came to my class, they were effusive. They had nothing but positive things to say and were pleased with my students' achievement, enthusiasm, and dynamics with me. Toward the end of their time in my classroom, I asked them about some hypothetical teaching best practices. I laid out both my method and the new approach handed down from the administration, plainly and without any sort of context. Just for kicks and giggles, really, to see what they thought. I had nothing to lose now.

You can guess what comes next.

*They sided with my approach.*

But my contract still wasn't renewed. So I moved on. I took my own children out of the school, and together, we went somewhere new. It's heartbreaking. I'm sad for our loss, yes, but my true sadness comes from the denigration of the educator's role and the compromised instruction I know other students at that school will experience. But I find hope in knowing that the other kindergarten teacher I worked with that year is still there. She is strong and she is tough, and she knows her stuff. She cares about her students, and she is doing the most good for them from within that toxic culture even today.

I consider this experience, though a momentous challenge, to also be a monumental victory. I grew so much as an educator and a person. I trusted myself and I spoke up for my students like I knew how. I have no regrets about what I did because no matter where I am, my mission is the same: to serve my students the best I can and to love them with abandon. And while there was no way I could've anticipated what would come, I'm excited for the future. Who knows what will come next?

## Path into Education

I was thirty-seven years old when I became a full-fledged teacher, with my own group of students and my own classroom. I've always loved education and learning and working with children, but my road to doing it as a career was nontraditional. I don't mind though. I think my winding path to teacher certification makes the day-to-day all the more rewarding for me. Teaching is something I'll never take for granted and will always protect for the sake of my students.

Small towns have their own charm, but often the resources available to their citizens are humble and scant. This limitation affects every facet of life, from business to education. As a result, when I became a senior in high school, I didn't believe college could possibly be in the cards for me. My family and I had very little money, and when I considered college, all I saw were dollar signs and costs we couldn't cover. I was smart, too. I was number three in my class, but there was only so much I could do. My school counselor didn't tell me about scholarship possibilities. I had no idea my high financial need was something I could overcome, a gap I could close—especially as a bright student. Because I didn't know, I didn't apply to college and enlisted in the military instead.

Knowledge is incredibly powerful. So is its lack.

It wasn't long before I returned home from the military due to health issues. When I got back, I married my high-school sweetheart, started studying business, and began a family. Two years into my business program, I was a mother of four and quickly realized I didn't want to try to juggle schoolwork and motherhood. So I stopped my studies a few hours short of my associate degree and raised my children. I'm so grateful I could give my kids my engaged, committed presence, but as they grew older, thoughts of school and finishing my degree kept coming back to me, until a moment at my kids' school sealed the deal.

"Work hard. Get smart. Graduate from college."

Appearing in promotional material, on posters in the hall, and on classroom walls, this was the school's guiding motto, an aspirational trajectory for students to shoot for. It gave them actionable goals they could work toward, and it culminated in a graduation experience beyond high school. Anyone could attend college, but not everyone graduates. Which is true in life, isn't it? It's easy to start something. You get excited about a new project or a new hobby you're ready to go all in on, but then time passes, life gets in the way, and that steam dissipates. After a while, all you have to show for your big idea is a pile of junk in the corner of that second bedroom you never touch anymore.

"Graduate from college." Suddenly, I was struck by the fact that I wanted this for my kids, and I also wanted it for myself. A switch flipped in me, and I couldn't turn it off. I wanted to graduate from college. This imperative pressed on me more and more, but the timing was never quite right to finish my degree. I kept looking for my opportunity, and then it appeared.

The company I worked for was undergoing some significant personnel changes, which made my position less assured and more tenuous. This was my chance. I quit my job and went back to school. My program was all online, which was a perfect fit for my life as a mother and a wife. Plus, I found part-time work that was flexible and accommodated my needs: I became a substitute teacher.

As my program went on, I kept subbing, eventually becoming a long-term sub for teachers who went on maternity leave or who had to be out for extended periods due to other reasons. I was a regular presence at the school and was with a single group of kids for up to eight weeks at a time. Teachers began requesting me by name to be their substitute—*me!*—and I grew more and more comfortable in the classroom setting. I could visualize myself being in the educational context for the long haul. I knew I wanted to be a teacher from then on. What could be better than being surrounded by the joyful delight of student discovery every day? What greater pleasure was there than spending your days with children, showing them love and helping them learn?

As soon as I graduated, I applied for an open teaching position at the school I had been subbing at for so long, which was also the school my own kids attended. And I didn't get it. Instead, I was hired on as a paraprofessional, but the next year, there was to be an available teaching position in the kindergarten, and I was hopeful that would be my next move.

I got it.

Now, I get to spend my days teaching children how to read and showing them I believe in them. I have the privilege of following in the footsteps of the beloved educators I had when I was an elementary student. My teaching approach and style is an amalgamation of all the best classroom instructors I enjoyed, mixed with my own personal flair. In me, there's a bit of Miss Ott, who was tall like an Amazon with gorgeous curly hair and dark, smoky glasses. Her lessons reached me more than most because she used a variety of methods and led us in competitions to learn and play. There's also a little of Ms. Peeples, who was crazy strict but loved us deeply and took us on the best field trips. However, my biggest teaching influence is probably Mrs. Oberley. She could fix you with a single look, and no one in the room would breathe. It would be so quiet you could hear a pin drop on a cotton swab. But on days where there were classroom parties, Mrs. Oberley's room was the place to be. The door was open, and every student was welcome. More than that, every student *wanted* to be in the room. It was full of life, and Mrs. Oberley was out among us, not reserved and hanging back behind her desk, letting us alone. Everything she did was in the students, of the students, and for her students. That's the sort of classroom and experience I strive to give my kids.

I know the undeniable influence that knowledge and education can have in a person's life. That's the kind of influence I've seen personally, and I want my students to see it, too. I want them to have all the facts, so they can choose their own path for the better. I want them to be confident and informed, so they can work hard, get smart, and graduate from college.

## Best Practice

*"I have no regrets about what I did because no matter where I am, my mission is the same: to serve my students the best I can and to love them with abandon. And while*

*there was no way I could've anticipated what would come, I'm excited for the future."*

More than any other, the first year of a teacher's career is a learning year. You are going to struggle, and that's okay. It's important to embrace that discomfort and learn from it. Sometimes, things won't turn out the way you hope or desire, but those are still opportunities for you to grow and evolve as an educator. Even though Tonya's instructional practices were correct and supported by the visiting literacy experts, her administration still let her go at the year's end. But she didn't give up, and she kept her main goal in sight.

It's not just the first year that's tough. Every year brings with it new challenges. When those hard days come, have a plan to help yourself stay positive and focused on what's most important: your kids' learning and well-being, and your own health and well-being. Make a short list every day of what went well and what didn't pan out as planned. What can you change next time for a better or different outcome? Be honest about your strengths and areas of improvement. When you search out and record the good moments as well as the challenging ones, you'll get quicker at recognizing them as they happen, and you won't get bogged down or overwhelmed by your perceived shortcomings. Keep your list daily for a week and on Friday, look back on it and see how it changes your perspective.

# Carmelita Shouldis

*Mission, South Dakota*

## Moment of Impact

Before I became an educator, I had one lens I looked through when it came to classroom teachers. In my experience, they were out of touch, sort of aloof, and definitely not interested in their students, let alone in standing up for them. For me. While I believed education could be a great thing, and was certainly an important thing, I didn't see its impact playing out much beyond the requisite tasks of grading, lecturing, managing classroom behavior, and occasionally meeting with parents or administrators. I didn't fully grasp the scope of what an educator does and who an educator can really be for a student. Until I became one, that is.

Because of the negative experiences I'd had in school, becoming a teacher or entering education in any way was never on my radar. It wasn't until I was recruited by Teach for America that my definition of "educator" expanded. I was sold on the idea that being an educator in the classroom meant being a leader—a trusted adult who would advocate for students, their health, their welfare, their empowerment. In theory, this was exciting and affirming, but I've found that in practice, this is harder than I could've imagined.

I was a first-year teacher and a Teach for America corps member. Since I hadn't studied education during undergrad, I received a lot of extra support, professional development, and guidance from TFA staff during my first two years in the classroom, in addition to the opportunities provided by my district. I was placed on a reservation in South Dakota and had the chance to teach third-grade students living on my own homelands. We shared a culture, an ancestry, and a bond that went deeper than just teacher-student. More than the obligation I felt to inform and support my students academically was the urgent sense of responsibility I felt to defend and champion them as Indigenous children, as members of my own tribe. I was surprised by the lengths to which the curriculum and teaching methods went to minimize the cultural identity of the Indigenous students and community, including me. I didn't understand how or why teachers who didn't live on the rez could dictate what the school's educational experience would look like.

Every day, my students and I confronted a racist culture in our building. When my principal observed my classes, my classroom management was criticized. My students weren't sitting still enough; they weren't attentive enough. In her opinion, their behavior warranted being sent out of the classroom to the hallway. I disagreed. I spoke with my principal and said my students were learning, but also, they were kids. Kids are wriggly. I didn't want to just dismiss them to the hall, sending them the message that they were too much to deal with and their learning wasn't worth my effort. I aimed to implement restorative practices with my students, but that wasn't what my administration wanted or expected.

Every time we reached a point of contention in my teaching practices or when damaging comments were made about my students, I spoke up. I tried to meet with my principal and discuss the issue directly. It was exhausting, but if I didn't work hard for my kids, who would? Eventually, my principal started avoiding me. Other teachers in the building did as well, even going so far as to cross to opposite sides of the hallway when they saw me coming. My principal opted out of making classroom visits herself and sent in other Indigenous faculty members, without my consent, because she perceived I was unwilling to have white people in my classroom. Ultimately, this conflict culminated in my being asked to relocate to another reservation school in the district. Fine by me.

Unfortunately, I quickly discovered these prejudices weren't confined to my former school site; they were widespread in the district and unavoidable. It was one thing for me to face them, the fear, the extra scrutiny, the averted gazes, but it was something else altogether for my students to endure.

A clear example of this was when my students repeatedly arrived to their physical education class later than the class schedule dictated. Literally, there was no time allotted for my students to pass from their prior period to PE, and they kept coming back to me, saying they got in trouble again for being late. I tried to help them see that they weren't "late," and it wasn't their fault the schedule was so tight. I didn't want them carrying guilt over something that was out of their hands, so I walked to PE with them the next time, believing I could speak to the teacher and clear up the misunderstanding. I explained to him that we had a period focused on Lakota culture immediately before PE, and I didn't want to cut that short just so we could arrive to the gym at the assigned time. My students learning about their culture, language, and heritage was essential and something I prioritized as often as I could. I apologized for the inconvenience but asked for a few minutes of leniency on my students' behalf.

We didn't get it.

Instead, he proceeded to shift his loud reprimand from my students to me, raising his voice at me in anger over the issue. When I brought this troubling incident to my administration, I received minimal support, which unfortunately was par for the course.

As early as September, my principal threatened to send letters home to my students' parents, warning them I wasn't a state-licensed educator (certification I was earning as part of my Teach for America commitment). No one at my school site came to my aid; my TFA mentors and managers did. My principal backed off, but the die had been cast for the school year, and I felt I had been marked as an outsider, even an undesirable, from the outset. This was exacerbated by my determination to advocate for and foster a deeper, more authentic engagement of Indigenous culture. On the surface, the school culture was indigenized, but when it came to genuine relationships with students and instruction regarding tribal values and practices, the school came up empty. I spoke out and fought for more—my students deserved more—and that set me apart.

My first two years in education were awful. I loved my students, and I did what I could to embody that ideal of leadership I found so inspiring, but the forces working against us in every aspect of our educational experience were daunting. Now, I'm at my third school site in three years, and I continue to be hopeful for the future. I continue to believe my community is capable of growth, learning, and grace. I still believe my students need someone to champion them, and it's my goal to be that advocate for them and their families, to help them learn the indigenous language, to preserve our shared heritage, to show them a path toward success, to love them, and to lead them. I've found that is the crux of what it means to be an educator: to be a strong leader who, no matter how many times you're pushed down, gets back up in front of their students to say, "I'll keep fighting for you. You are worth the fight."

## Path into Education

When it comes to people and their careers, some people grow up knowing what they want to be. They saw a positive example of a person performing a job or existing within a profession, and they want to emulate that in their own adulthood, attracted by the prestige, the money, or the purpose associated with it. Some people grow up knowing what they *don't* want to do for a career, often because of the inverse of the above conditions. They had poor experiences with a person in a given role, and now that profession is sullied for them or in desperate need of redemption. That's me.

As a student, my school experience was bad. I was bullied pretty severely in elementary school, though things improved a little as I got older. A handful of boys had me in their sights for who knows what reason. They would hit me, call me names, pull my hair, whatever they could do to make me miserable. To make me feel like I didn't belong and wasn't wanted at school. When I defended myself and fought back, I got in trouble. In second grade, one of my tormenters, Dax, slammed my head into a desk, and the substitute teacher who saw it happen just stood by. My family decided I should attend boarding school to get me out of these terrible situations. The time away was fine though uneventful, but I dreaded returning to my hometown and the faces of the friends and bullies I'd left behind. When I came back in seventh grade, Dax was there, and we reentered our drama right where we'd left off.

"Back from treatment, I see."

"I thought you were coming back for high school. That's when I was planning to transfer."

"Why are you even here?"

Ultimately, Dax did transfer. Evidently, he wanted to be in school with me as much as I wanted to be in school with him. Once he was gone, the rest of my schooling passed without consequence, but I had a bad taste in my mouth. Not only had I been mistreated by fellow students, but I also felt utterly neglected and misunderstood by my teachers. They were completely wack, totally disconnected from me and my classmates in every way. I didn't see myself in them, which is unsurprising since most of my teachers weren't Indigenous and lived off the rez, driving in from other parts of town to work each day. I didn't view them as advocates, supporters, or even as adults I could trust. School and everything about it was something I had to survive. There was nothing comforting, validating, or meaningful there for me. Nothing enticing to come back for, I thought.

As a senior in college, I started thinking about the future. I wasn't sure where I was heading after graduation, but I had several passions: public health and welfare, and raising awareness around social and emotional health. I didn't know where these interests would fit in for me career-wise, but I wasn't too stressed yet, even though some of my friends already had clear paths marked for themselves. One of them had committed to Teach for America, a nonprofit organization that trains and places high-performing individuals in low-income communities to teach at local schools. You didn't have to be an education major to be selected for TFA, apparently, so I went along to a meet-and-greet with my friend, telling her explicitly I wasn't interested and was there only because she invited me. That, and the free food.

During the event, we heard TFA staff members talk about the mission of the organization (to provide an excellent and equitable education for all children) and their understanding of what makes an effective educator in the classroom. Most of what they discussed was about leadership and how being a strong educator is really about being a strong leader who is willing to fight for students and stand up to injustice. I was surprised. This was not a description that was consistent with the educators I'd interacted with during my time in school on the rez. It characterized the sort of people I wish I'd had in my corner when I was a bullied student who felt alone and out of place. Here was an organization that said its goal was to prioritize actual leadership, empathy, courage, diversity, and inclusion—values I appreciated.

My interest was piqued, but I still didn't see myself as a person who could stand up in front of a classroom and tell kids what to do. That's something that had been done to me. It was not something I wanted to do to others. However, eventually, the executive director of Teach for America South Dakota reached out to me specifically. The families on the Rosebud Indian Reservation had expressed a desire to have more Indigenous educators in the classroom teaching their Indigenous students. As a Native woman, I was being recruited, and I was wary. The doubt and shadow from my past lingered. I didn't want to be another teacher like those I'd had.

"We don't want you to be like that either," the director told me. "The things you're interested in, public health and care in low-income communities, are causes you can work toward and integrate into the classroom. You can be the advocate for your students that you never had. You're a leader. Teaching is about leadership. Bring that leadership and passion to your classroom."

This conversation opened my eyes to see that there was more to education than just my single experience. Even though I hadn't seen myself in any of the educators I'd grown up with, I could still be an educator. I could reshape what it meant to be an educator, and I could have a part in ensuring healthy, positive outcomes and experiences for my students. I could make my classroom a place of affirmation and rigor, and I could educate my students on things beyond academics. I could make an impact and have an even deeper impact on the rez, working to help students and their families learn more about our nation's heritage, culture, language, and identity.

So yeah, I did kind of find myself in a profession I never expected, but I'm so glad I've landed here. I'm so glad I get to be the kind of teacher I wanted to have. I'm thankful to have the chance to be the kind of educator my students really deserve.

## Best Practice

*"My students learning about their culture, language, and heritage was essential and something I prioritized as often as I could."*

As educators, we have the opportunity not only to set academic goals for students and equip them to achieve those goals, but we also have the chance to address more intangible outcomes, like building self-confidence, vision, and independence. A crucial part of being an educator is instilling within students the abilities to trust themselves and to know who they are and where they come from. Like Carmelita, there are concrete ways to make space for this in the classroom by soliciting students' opinions and feedback on lesson plans, unit objectives, and more.

The next time you're beginning to brainstorm an upcoming unit or the next time your lesson plans for the day get interrupted, ask students for their input. Hear what they think is important and what they want to accomplish in the upcoming hour, weeks, or months. Then incorporate that feedback into what you execute if it makes sense with your overall plan. Validate their identity and voice by valuing them more highly in your instructional approaches. You'll be surprised by how insightful and compelling their suggestions can be.

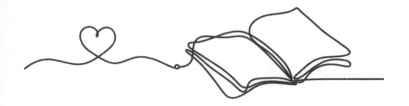

# Lorena Lopez

*Hammond, Indiana*

## Moment of Impact

There are two sides to every story, two halves to every dialogue, and always more than one way to look at a situation. This is especially true when it comes to history, a field whose narrative is spun by the winners only. It's also true in language and communication when the listener can hear a very different message from what the speaker meant to convey. Interpretation is subjective yet powerful, which makes it dangerous and slippery.

An example.

I had an eighth-grade student named Israel I was supporting as he worked on a US history test. The historical event he and his class were studying at the time was the Texas Revolution, particularly the Battle of the Alamo. Israel was from Mexico and had just arrived in the United States. In Mexico, he'd been taught his country's history, its significant moments, and its turning points. Fortunately, the Alamo and its surrounding conflict was something he'd learned about already, so he felt equipped and confident to tackle this material. We worked on translating the test questions together, and he dove into the answers. He completed the test and turned it in, proud of his hard work and believing he'd answered the questions completely and accurately.

When Israel got his grade back, he saw a big fat zero. *What*?

I reviewed his answers once again, looking for errors and inaccuracies that would warrant such a disastrous result of his diligent effort. The more time I spent with his test, the questions, and his answers, the more I began to uncover the truth.

Israel had grown up without any background or instruction in US history as it was taught in the American educational system. So, while he had answered the questions accurately, his answers represented the Mexican perspective of the Battle. This was the point of view he was accustomed to, the one he understood best. It eventually became clear that Israel's teacher was looking for answers that more clearly reflected the opposing view: the American perspective of the conflict. She wanted responses that were consistent with the instruction provided by the textbook. In other words, she accepted answers validating the victor's perspective instead of the conquered party's perspective.

Israel's answers were inconvenient and maybe uncomfortable, but they most certainly were correct.

I pushed back.

I spoke with the teacher, and she proved intractable in her stance, so I went to the department chair and school leader for additional support. In looking at the teacher's grading rubric, there were no criteria explicitly preventing Israel from receiving the credit he deserved. Eventually, the social studies teacher was made to accept Israel's answers—she was *made* to accept his completely accurate, hard-fought answers—but after the issue was resolved, she changed her rubric so that in the future, student answers must explicitly adhere to and reflect the content as laid out in the textbook. Israel had won this battle, but unfortunately, the conditions changed afterward to make the war more impossible for other students to overcome.

Isn't this exactly what learning about history warns against?

In my experience working with English language learners, these kinds of attitudes are ever present. My students are beginning from a place of challenge and disadvantage, and if they just recently arrived in the US and the American school system, those difficulties are even more pronounced. Not only must they learn a foreign language that's full of linguistic exceptions and changeable laws, but they also must learn how to survive in a system and a society that is founded upon those same inconsistencies. It's my job, my honor, and my imperative to help them walk through it and make it to the other side ... even when there's no guarantee anything will be different once they get there. I want to give them the tools, so they know how and when to use them to be successful and fulfilled.

As in most things, there is no one-size-fits-all approach in education. In life, there is rarely ever just one way to accomplish something, and when you're engaging with a second or third language, that's even truer. But I like to see this perspective in my students because I suppose I view things from that vantage point as well. When things don't come naturally, you work harder at them, but you're also better equipped to see different sides of an issue and adopt a more creative, unconventional approach to the challenge.

That's the essence of what I do in my role. I enter teachers' classrooms to provide one-on-one language support to students as needed. Having been relegated to the back corners of classrooms, neglected and ignored by instructors, and looked down upon for the inconvenience I am, I've grown accustomed to the resistance language learners face in education. For whatever reason these negative attitudes fester, the crux of the issue is that teachers must contend with something foreign and unfamiliar in their classroom. The language is unknown to them, my instructional practices are different from theirs, the grading standards and conventions require more flexibility or accommodation, etc.

The curious thing is, that's exactly what my students are doing with English, except they don't have the option to bend the rules or wish them away. They have to push through and keep working until they succeed, and it's a joy to witness those triumphant moments and breakthroughs.

While some classroom teachers are welcoming and extremely receptive and open minded to my presence and my students' needs, this example with Israel is one I think about a lot. It helps me remember that sometimes the non-Spanish-speaking educators I work with need my support and encouragement, too. It helps me remember that there is always more than one way to do something, and it pushes me to find new methods and avenues of learning for my students. Education, language, and cultural narratives evolve and are always more complex than we think. Reflecting on Israel and the discrepancies between the stories history-makers can tell reminds me to invite more voices into the conversation, even if they're not speaking the same language.

## Path into Education

All educators act as a bridge to help students get from where they are to where they need to be. We help students learn new skills and master the necessary objectives and vocabulary to progress to the next level and gain success in the future. However, for the students I serve—and for me, when I was a student—the gap between the starting point and the goal destination is much wider.

I work with English language learners and support them in first grasping the English language, so they are then capable to comprehend and master the subject-area material. I do this work because it's important but also because it's personal. When I was a newcomer to the United States as a seven-year-old, I had no instructional supports to help me navigate my new school or this new language of English. I was dropped into the second grade without a clue how to communicate, let alone learn what was taught.

My family and I moved to Chicago from Mexico, and the change was drastic. I entered the Chicago Public School system, a massive, sprawling district that would have been intimidating even if I had grown up in the city. Everything about the move was difficult and jarring. When I arrived at school, there were no English Language Learning (ELL) classes for me to enroll in or language specialists who could supplement instruction and support me in my classwork. I did my best, but it was like trying to fell a tree with a spoon; I didn't have the appropriate tools. I had absolutely no understanding of English phonetics and could only crudely imitate sounds. When I attempted to speak English, I was mocked for my errors and grew more and more ashamed and embarrassed. I couldn't practice at home because my parents wanted me to speak Spanish exclusively. I couldn't imagine how things would improve for me without a change.

Fortunately, Ms. Butler found me.

Ms. Butler wasn't a Spanish speaker. She was my English teacher and saw my struggle. While she herself didn't have the resources I needed linguistically, she knew how to point me in the right direction, and she was able to secure some additional help for me. She recommended I take a diagnostic instructional test in Spanish, my native language, to assess the grade level of my natural skills without the barrier of a foreign language. As it turned out, I tested at the fourth-grade level, and my school administrators promoted me out of second grade and into fourth. While learning English was still an ongoing process for me, I began making small improvements. Most importantly, though, I now had the relief and affirmation of knowing I wasn't stupid. My struggles weren't a result of my inability to learn or some mental block preventing me from connecting the dots. I just didn't know the language. At last, my teachers knew I was actually smart; I just didn't have a means to communicate my knowledge.

I was standing in front of that obstinate tree, and someone finally handed me a saw.

Once in the fourth grade, I began to improve steadily. It wasn't an overnight transformation, but the diagnostic and its subsequent placement worked wonders for my confidence. I was more hopeful and optimistic. I gradually made friends. As my language skills accelerated, the tension at home defused. I had more opportunities to practice English at school and was better equipped to do so, which allowed me to honor my parents' rules and retain hope at the same time.

Because of the difficulties of my own journey with language learning, I was determined to become an educator to alleviate those same burdens my students face today.

Today, I work in the language department as an ELL educator, directly supporting and advocating for students whose first (and in some cases, second) language is not English, the language of their instruction. I go into subject-area classrooms and provide supplemental supports for students who need additional language accommodations. My goal is to facilitate English comprehension, utilizing both Spanish and English, so that students can approach their academic material from a place of strength.

While this work is tough and comes with its own set of challenges, I see its impact. More than that, I see my own familiar struggle in my students. It's not only the mechanics of English we wrestle with. We also battle the misperceptions of my students' intelligence. Mixing up verb tenses or conjugating incorrectly can be viewed as evidence of a lesser intelligence or a lack of effort rather than what it is: a minor (and expected) error arising from translation. My students do twice the work and feel sometimes like they receive only half the recognition or validation other students get. I remember how that feels and that's why I stay in the classroom. I love my students and I want them to succeed, so I do what I can to help them along that road, including educating their families when appropriate.

Learning a language is a holistic, immersive experience, and my students' families often struggle with English as well. That, or they don't feel comfortable in the educational setting. They feel disempowered, so I try to make them aware of the school and community services available to them. The school counselors and I team up to host parent nights to inform parents and guardians about scholarships and other resources that can make a difference for them and their students.

When I was a student arriving in an English-speaking country, city, and school for the first time, I needed someone who thought outside of the academic box to help me move forward. That's what I try to bear in my mind with my students, too. Education is a comprehensive, whole-person endeavor. It's not enough to give students the linguistic tools to recognize and speak foreign words. What they and their families need is someone ready to help bolster their confidence, to direct them toward available resources and supports, and to view them as complete, whole individuals. Language mastery is the key that unlocks all the rest of those doors of learning, and it's a privilege to place that power in students' hands.

## Best Practice

*"There are two sides to every story, two halves to every dialogue, and always more than one way to look at a situation."*

It's imperative to remember that every story has multiple vantage points, in the same way that every student has numerous factors affecting them in the classroom. Lorena experienced this with Israel and his social studies teacher. She also experienced this with a Guatemalan student whose native tongue was an indigenous Mayan language, second language was Spanish, and third language was English. Isabela was struggling with her Spanish literacy, and after a while, Lorena discovered that Isabela had been out of the educational system for six years, her parents were deported almost immediately after she and her family arrived in the US, and she was now in the foster care system. No wonder she was struggling.

Understanding where students are starting from is critical in serving them effectively in the classroom. Identify a student encountering consistent academic challenges in your class. Set aside time each week to get to know them better, so you can see the full picture of where they are and why they might be having a hard time learning the material. What might you be missing from their story that could help you tailor your instruction to their needs?

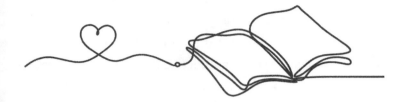

# Roxana Dueñas

*Los Angeles, California*

## Moment of Impact

I nadequate pay. Unsustainable class sizes. Insufficient, or nonexistent, support-staff resources. Neglect and marginalization in deference to more affluent school districts.

As an educator, you know these pain points far too well. And you've likely acclimated to them and adapted to serve your students in spite of these limitations because if you don't, who will? Those of us who work in education are well-versed in challenges like these, with many of us receiving the message from district administrators that things can't or won't change. So when there's an opportunity to fight for improvements to our districts and for the welfare of our students, there's no question of whether or not to seize the moment. And that's what my colleagues and I did in 2019.

The defining moment of my career was when I participated in the 2019 Los Angeles Unified School District teachers' strike.

In my history and ethnic studies class, my students and I regularly study historical events and figures that center around resistance movements, civil disobedience, and fighting for one's rights. It's one thing to study these concepts, lecture on them, and even encourage students to join those movements. It's another to join them yourself. We tell students all the time, "You can do it." The strike was a moment when I had to confront myself: *Can I do it? Can* we *do it?*

When the time finally came for the district's teachers to physically leave our classrooms and protest for our and our students' rights, it was almost unbelievable. In many ways, we had been organizing and preparing for this for over two years. It wasn't until we were actually out there in the streets, holding our signs, seeing students coming to support us at the picket lines, that I finally realized, *This is what a social movement looks like. This is the reality of collective action. This is his-*

*tory in the making.* It was terrifying and empowering at the same time.

Throughout that season of the movement—because, of course, the broader movement toward equity, dignity, and power in education continues daily in our classrooms—I came to understand the interconnectedness of the educator community in an entirely new way. There were over 30,000 of us across the LAUSD who took part in the strike. No one of us could have made that impact on our own. It took all of us together, side by side, working hard toward the same goal for our demands to be met and the collective voice of educators across our district to be heard. This was inexpressibly powerful, and it still is something I look back on and point to as a fundamental shift in my approach to education and who I am as an educator.

So much of what we do as teachers is done in isolation. You remain at your school site, within your grade level, your department, and in your classroom. The strike dismantled those divisions and united us across all subjects, ages, and school sites. Looking next to me, I would see on one side a nurse from an elementary school across town, and on my other side, I'd see a librarian who served junior-high students at a school just a few blocks away. The impact of that solidarity is beyond words. It was so humanizing and affirming. We each recognized that our work does matter and the challenges and frustrations we face on our own are not individual issues at all. The strike embodied that reality. It was a physical representation of this idea: We collectively agree that we're all struggling with the same issues. It's not just me. We're all facing conditions and demands that are unfair and unjustifiable.

The strike gave me a chance to practice what I teach. It was a once-in-a-lifetime culmination of the lessons I revisit with my students day in and day out, things we tell students to do but traits we as adults don't practice enough. Courage. Humility. Collaboration with others. We all need each other. Educators need students, and we need our fellow educators. Teaching is an arduous privilege, an honorable challenge, and finding meaningful community to walk through that journey alongside has been crucial for me. I'm thankful for a lot of what followed after the strike, and a newfound camaraderie with and appreciation for my colleagues throughout the district is chief among them. While we were all members of the same school district, it didn't feel that way. The second-largest district in the state of California, LAUSD is spread far and wide, making it hard to truly grasp a sense of unity. Through the strike, we could embrace the fact that we are a single entity for the first time. We demonstrated as one, pushed back against injustice as one, and elevated the needs and rights of our students and ourselves as one community. One collective body disrupting for a higher purpose.

What we didn't expect was to see another school district in the state follow our example. The Oakland school district had been watching our strike and the efforts leading up to it and modeled its own resistance after ours. What a humbling experience to not only do something to fight for my students but also to have indirectly paved the way for other educators to fight for their own students. All our apparently separate efforts and initiatives are inextricably tied to one another. The work we do in one district and for one student body spills over into others and ultimately helps create a stronger, healthier educational system in our state. If it can happen statewide, why can't it happen nationwide? We're in the midst of a movement. A rising tide lifts all ships.

It's pretty heady to know that in 2019, I wasn't merely teaching history. My fellow educators and I were creating it. Someday many years from now, other students in other classrooms will be reading about this teachers' strike. I hope they'll be inspired to take action and work together to implement change, to innovate, and to challenge the systems that no longer serve them. And I'm thrilled to see the history-making trails they will blaze in their own futures.

## Path into Education

You can't be what you can't see.

Milbrey Wallin McLaughlin brought this concept into the mainstream in her 2018 book bearing this phrase as its title. In recent years, the idea of mirroring has gained traction in the broader conversation. While this sentiment is certainly true on one level, it can be limiting in other respects. You can be a powerful trailblazer and a boundary-breaker when no one like you has been before. Nonetheless, the essence of this notion is what drove me to education, and the ideas of setting an example and living out the principles I teach still guide me in my instructional practices today.

As a student, my educational experience was distinct from my peers. As an elementary student, I was an English language learner who did not have a bilingual teacher in my classrooms. My parents were immigrants, so my family and I spoke only Spanish, which made my initial years in the English-speaking classroom incredibly difficult. To adjust to a new school and new classmates already feels insurmountable to a kid; to attempt that transition on your own, without any verbal support or facilitation from the adults you see at your school every day, makes that challenge even more daunting. But time passed, as it does. I worked hard, picked things up, and eventually, I learned English fluently and entered secondary school.

After conquering the language barrier, I had supportive teachers who encouraged and pushed me during junior high and high school. I enrolled in honors courses and was on the honors track toward college. I didn't realize until later how different my educational experience was from some of my classmates. I couldn't broaden my perspective enough to grasp how rigid and traditionally informed the American educational system was until much later. While I'd had a positive and valuable experience as a student, I had no idea how small my purview was. Arriving at college liberated me.

My time at university prompted me to question what I had known and believed up to that point. About everything. Rather than being told what to think, I was shown how to think and how to question what I encountered in my courses. Everything was pliable. Nothing was off limits to change or challenge. I felt as though I had turned around to see the shadows on the cave wall for what they really were—props and implements of reality—and I was gaining the ability to effect change and influence the future autonomously and on my own terms. I experienced the power of education and knowledge in a brand-new way and never wanted to lose it again. I wanted to leverage it to create a new version of learning and an alternative way of existing in the world. This led me to study history, and when I entered the classroom as an educator, I rooted my approach in learning from the past in order to reimagine the future.

I teach history and ethnic studies, and I aim to lead my students to question everything. The textbooks they read: Who wrote them? What version of these historical events are we receiving? What voices are not represented in this account? Why are some experiences neglected or omitted? What can we disrupt to create a more inclusive system, a more inclusive world?

My students and I are embedded in these kinds of questions every day. Traditional American schooling can be quite a colonial project, and it can rob students—and educators—of imagination, originality, and that natural spark of curiosity we feel when our interests align with our studies. I don't want my students to feel like they have to fit into any sort of mold. I want them to be self-aware enough to destroy *all* the templates the culture tries to push on them and to be empowered enough to manifest the society and experience and world they want to live in! Regardless of the field my students intend to enter after high school or higher education, I want them ready to interrupt and interrogate what they see and what the status quo suggests is immutable. Everything is changeable, but we must believe in that change and have agency to do something about it. We must understand that other possibilities exist and that the way things are is not how they must always be, or even how they should be.

I began my journey with education as an isolated, disoriented student who was nonetheless eager to learn and be included. Now, I try to craft my classroom environment and lessons to meet students with similar feelings right where they are and bring them into the conversation. I want all my students to feel welcome and know they have something meaningful and unique to contribute. Hopefully then, they will grasp the truth that they deserve a seat at the table, and if the table won't accommodate them, they can walk away and dream up a new place to sit. From time to time, I wonder what kind of person I would have been if my teachers had encouraged me to deeply question and interrogate like this before I arrived at university. Who could I have been if I had been cognizant and critical of the institutional and ideological oppression so many students face—that I myself was facing? What version of myself would I now be if I'd had the tools to call into question those systems and philosophies that weren't, and still aren't, working?

My own experience as a student fuels and informs my approach as an educator. I'm always asking how I can create space for inquiry and open-ended questions. I'm constantly looking for opportunities to develop a practice of curiosity within my students, so they can chase the things that excite them and research those that don't sit well with them. I want my students to forge and discover their own knowledge and pursue it independently rather than merely receive passed-down instruction from another person. I don't want my students to wonder about who they may have been if they had only known what they were missing.

As a student, I was told why. As an educator, I help students *ask* why. When I get the chance, I try to find new ways I can practice disruption by dismantling what's broken and building something whole that will serve everyone inclusively and equitably.

I became an educator to be the teacher I never had.

## Best Practice

*"Educators need students, and we also need our fellow educators. Teaching is an arduous privilege, an honorable challenge, and finding meaningful community to walk through that journey alongside has been crucial for me."*

As an educator, it's easy to hole up in your classroom, within the safety of your subject area, and stay there. But it's crucial to go outside your comfort zone and to build meaningful relationships with other educators. Discomfort and stretching are the places where growth happens. Like Roxana experienced in the LAUSD teachers' strike, the work we do and the goals we want to achieve are supercharged and far more likely to be realized when working together with others. Seek inspiration from others' lessons and share your own. Ask for support and resources from seasoned teachers you respect. Visit classrooms and observe other educators at work. You don't have to reinvent the wheel, and you don't have to strive by yourself. Find your people and endeavor together!

Think of an educator you admire in your building or district. Set aside time to observe them in their classroom or to talk with them about their favorite lessons. What strategies are they using that you can apply in your own instruction? Incorporate an idea from another professional into your lesson plans this month, this unit, or even this week.

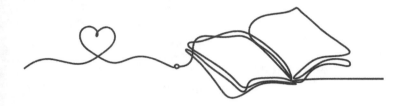

# Amy Crawford
*Maryville, Tennessee*

## Moment of Impact

You know those times that split your life into a Before and an After? Something that changes you so fundamentally, you can clearly trace where the path diverged and led you to the road you're on today?

I want to tell you that story.

I had been teaching for several years. At last, I was in that comfortable, confident space where you feel yourself getting in the groove, well beyond the first-year pains but still as excited and energized as you were at the beginning. The more self-assured and competent I became, the better a teacher I became. There's never really a time when you've "made it" in education. You're always learning and growing, figuring out new technology (I'm looking at you, Zoom), researching new instructional methods, reinventing lesson plans to incorporate current events or other things that are relevant to students. But I felt established in my career and really joyful in my profession. Around this time, my district approached me and asked if I would participate in an experiment they had in mind.

The idea was to pair the highest-performing teachers, as decided by some tests the previous year (don't get me started on standardized testing as an accurate means of evaluation), with students in the lowest-performing schools for two years. No system is perfect, let alone any educator, but I was interested. I've always believed teaching to be my vocation. It's something I knew was meant for me, even when I didn't want to acknowledge it, but once I did, education had me hook, line, and sinker. This was my mindset, and I wanted to do all that was in my power to educate and love as many students as I could. So I said yes.

I was placed in a low-income school teaching fourth grade. There were fourteen students in my class, and each of them had their own unique story of challenge.

All of them qualified for free or reduced lunch, most of them came from unstable or disrupted home situations, and every one of them was full of passion and ... *spirit*. They were a rowdy bunch of firecrackers who needed more than I was able to give them, but I did my utmost to see them, treasure them, and teach them during our time together. While they fought hard with each other and with me, they loved in equal measure, and I was continually surprised by how fun and compassionate they were. There is one moment, however, when they downright shocked me.

One day, we were in our portable classroom at the rear of the building, and I was talking to my students about how the next school day they were going to have a substitute teacher with them instead of me. Naturally, my kids wanted to know why. I needed to go into the doctor's office, which—of course—prompted another *Why?*

"Well, I found a place on my skin. I'm not sure what it is, so I'm going to have the doctor check it out just in case. But I have to admit, I'm really nervous about it."

Just then, one of my students, Jason, stood up and announced to the class, "All right, everybody. We gon' pray for Coach Crawford. Y'all circle up and bow your heads."

I was flabbergasted. He was a student who had some of the greatest difficulty controlling his behavior, often talking out of turn in class and drawing attention to himself during our lessons. Now, he was leading the class in one of the sweetest, most sincere prayers I've ever heard. Jason prayed I would have peace, the doctor would have wisdom, and everything would turn out okay. I was humbled and moved more than words. Those students and those years changed me.

There are a lot of times when education is so much more than, and sometimes everything but, teaching. This class, and those two years, are a testament to that. My students needed to learn and be prepared for fifth grade, but they needed so much more. They needed love, attention, and tenderness. When other colleagues or friends of mine heard about the district's experiment and learned some of the details of where I was and the community I was serving, they typically expressed some variation of, "How wonderful. Think of all you're doing for them." They have it backwards, though. It's my students who do so much for me. They make me want to be a better person. Knowing their eyes are on me and they're watching to see how I'll respond to a classroom outburst or a spilled coffee or an unkind word keeps me honest. It helps me aspire to be the sort of person I hope they become. They help me get closer to the sort of person *I* hope to become!

My students are the core of everything I do, and the privilege of showing up for them every morning and spending our days together is one I do not take for granted. Every day is filled with memorable moments and little victories. You just have to look for them. And every student is filled with untapped potential and unexplored depths. But you have to work for it.

I like to think of each of my kids as an island full of buried treasure. At the beginning of the school year, you're presented with all these new, unfamiliar landscapes. You have daily opportunities to learn them, figure out their boundaries, observe where the hills rise and the valleys dip, what kinds of days bring what sorts of weather. Slowly, you start to dig around a little, and after a while, your persistence is rewarded. You discover nuggets you didn't know were there. From moment to moment, kids will delight and surprise you with their kindness, wit, brilliance, and gentleness. "I didn't know you had that in you!" What a joy. What an honor it is to go on that adventure with students each day and begin again the next school year.

Those two years were tough, but I wouldn't trade them for the world. They reshaped my perspectives on education and student-teacher dynamics. I have the privilege of experiencing life at my students' sides and being a faithful presence in their days. I get to walk through a year of their lives with them. Daily, I get to watch the good, the bad, and everything in between unfold.

As an educator, I know *I'm* the lucky one.

## Path into Education

Your decisions shape your future.

This is a mantra in my classroom. It's up on a poster on the wall. It's a refrain my students hear from me all the time. They even hear it from each other, accompanied by only the occasional eye roll. While they may tire of hearing this phrase, my hope is that they internalize its meaning. I want them to remember the power and impact of their decisions on whatever they choose to pursue or study or dedicate themselves to in life. Here's a recent example.

I handed out a homework assignment, which was met with the typical weeping and gnashing of teeth.

"Ugh, Coach Crawford, do we *have* to do this homework?"

Unfazed, I looked at them and smiled, "Absolutely not," a response that elicited jubilation and cheers. Freedom! "Although, you know," I paused, "your decisions shape your future. Deciding to do your homework shows discipline. And you need discipline in life. Especially if you want to play in the NFL or be a musician." I met the eyes of our aspiring football stars and singers. Gnashing resumed, now accompanied by grumbling.

These are the moments that keep me in education. It's these opportunities to speak life to my students and help widen their perspectives and understanding of their own agency that call me back day after day.

I come from a family of educators, and my grandfather in particular showed me the potency and beauty of learning, of literature, of poetry. A longtime elementary principal, he took his time with me when I was young and regularly read aloud to me. Even all these years later, I still remember the sound of the book spines cracking, the sight of him licking his fingertip to turn the corner of a page, and the warm, dusty smell of the covers and pages as they fell open. I had two sisters: one of them was gorgeous, and one of them was athletic. While they had the spotlight, I had my grandpa, and together, we had our books. These are memories I cherish fondly, but even so, I didn't automatically want to be a teacher from the get-go.

I avoided education for a long time, even though I was in close proximity to it. We were like dance partners circling one another all evening before finally meeting for the last dance. As an undergrad, I thought advertising would be a good spot for me, thinking my future was to capture people's attention through jingles and ad slogans. It wasn't. When I took some exploratory courses in education, I knew I'd finally found my inevitable match, a space I felt was tailored perfectly for me. Like a hand in a glove.

From then on, I knew I had found my calling. I am certain education is what I am designed to do. If I ever have any doubt, my students dispel it every day. They deserve every opportunity to have the sort of futures and lives they want, and part of that comes from having committed, knowledgeable teachers. It comes from having teachers who are dedicated to students' well-being and who don't simply toss students out of the classroom when they get upset. It comes from interacting with teachers who are forgiving and honest about their own flaws and who show students they can be that way, too. They can be themselves. They don't have to put on a show in front of others, and they don't have to be afraid when they make mistakes or feel strong emotions. Students need adults like this, and while I can't be all things to all people at all times—and as an educator, this is an illusion I was quickly disabused of—I can show up and be a consistent presence in the classroom. I can be there for my students, so they in turn will be there for themselves.

Your decisions shape your future.

The decisions today's students make will shape *our* future. It's my goal to give them the things they need, like critical thinking, yes, but also self-worth and trusting their gut, to form that future for themselves. Not to have it decided for them by another person, another system, or the neglect thereof. Stepping into a role of influence for young people is a weighty responsibility that never goes away, which is why I'll work for it as long as I can. I try to help my students practice this in the classroom. They'll finish an in-class activity or complete a task and ask me what I think of it.

"What do you think of it?" I always ask them. "If it's good enough for you, who cares what I think? Your opinion is the one that matters most. You're the one that needs to be happy with yourself and what you've done, not me." I want to equip my students to take ownership of their futures and to have high standards for themselves. Asking them these silly-seeming questions is part of that, but the pursuit of self-actualization is one of the most serious they'll undertake all their lives. I want to prepare them, so they're ready to do that when it's time.

This isn't just a lesson for my students, though. These practices in my classroom reinforce the same ideas and instill the same qualities in me. My decisions affect my life and give way to my future. I've seen this play out in countless ways, not just in my decision to pursue the educational profession but also in the decisions nested within my role as educator. Being present for my students and pouring myself out for them emotionally and physically all day took a toll on me as a young mother. Something a lot of potential educators don't think about is how this outpouring on behalf of other people's children will affect your capacity to love and serve your own. I was confronted by this as a parent. Once my daughters were older, I apologized for all the times I couldn't give them everything I wanted because I was so depleted by the end of the school day. I apologized for the evenings I attended students' activities and missed my own kids' goings-on. And my girls understood. They can see I was making the best decisions I could to love and care for all my kids, not just my biological children. Now, one of my daughters is going into education, and she understands this practice from the inside out.

Our choices matter, and they can make a huge difference in the life of a child.

Every action has consequences, and when I wake up every morning, I know I'm doing something that matters. At the end of my life, I don't want to have regrets about the work I did, the opportunities I had, or the lives I've touched.

## Best Practice

*"Being present for my students and pouring myself out for them emotionally and physically all day took a toll on me as a young mother. Something a lot of potential educators don't think about is how this outpouring on behalf of other people's children will affect your capacity to love and serve your own. I was confronted by this as a parent. I apologized to my daughters once they got older for the times I couldn't give them all I wanted because I was so depleted at the end of the school day."*

The classroom experience isn't how it's depicted in the media. There is no movie that illustrates its totality authentically, and there is nothing that fully prepares you for all that awaits in the trenches. Enter your building and your classroom day after day, but especially that first day, knowing you will need to give yourself grace, as well as your students, parents, and administrators. You will mess up—no one is perfect—and it's okay. Don't carry those mistakes with you. Learn from them, move forward, and tend to your mental and emotional energy reserves.

Honestly evaluate the amount of time, effort, and emotional resources you expend in service of your students. What do you have remaining for yourself? For your family? Your hobbies? If burnout is close, or if you're already there, seriously consider where you can healthfully scale back in order to make more conscious, restful investments in your own mental health and care. Reallocate an hour every day, or every week if you need to start slow, away from school- or student-related responsibilities and toward yourself and your loved ones. How does that habit change your relationships? How does it change you?

# Jackie Mancinelli

*Voorhees Township, New Jersey*

## Moment of Impact

My identity is embedded in who I am as an educator. These two things cannot be disentangled. I am Jackie. I am a wife to my high school sweetheart. I am a mother to two beautiful daughters. I'm a former soccer player. And I am an educator. It's who I have been and who I always will be. Some people advise against this in favor of a clean separation between their work and personal selves, but education is part of my essence. I savor it, and I am grateful for its prominent role in shaping my identity. My existence in the classroom has been the one constant in my life, and my relationships with students have given me a soft place to land when tough times trip me up and I fall. And when I was early in my teaching career, I fell hard.

In September of 2015, I lost my father unexpectedly. Shortly after, I discovered I was pregnant with a son, and as I had no brothers, it was special to know I would be able to carry on my father's legacy through my son. It was the beginning of the school year, and it wasn't long before my students realized I was pregnant. Young people are extremely perceptive. They pay attention, and once I announced my pregnancy and confirmed their suspicions about my flowing tops and loose skirts, they became my biggest supporters. They wouldn't let me move furniture. They cautioned me when I made sudden movements. One student, Scott, checked on me every day, asking how I was feeling and was I doing all right. My students and their parents gave me gifts and planned a baby shower for me. They were with me every step of my pregnancy, literally, as my nine months and the length of school year aligned.

One day at school when I was around thirty-three weeks along, I experienced a lot of back pain. I knew it was too early for my son, Richard, to arrive, so I didn't think too much about it, but it was noticeable enough for me to sit down. An educator's day is spent on their feet, walking up and down between students' desks, leading activities, or presenting material at the front of the room. When I had to sit down, Scott—my diligent monitor—picked up on something foreboding before I did. I went through the day as usual but decided to visit the doctor that evening just to be safe. What I didn't know until later was that I had gone into pre-term labor. Those pains I felt that entire school day were labor pains.

I called my husband, who left work in a flurry anticipating Richard's early arrival, and I was admitted to the hospital as the nurses and doctors ran tests on both the baby and myself. After Richard failed all the tests assessing his health and activity, my team decided I needed to undergo an emergency C-section. After he was delivered, I looked up to see that the NICU team had doubled in size, making the room impossibly small, and I learned there had been a lot of blood. More than there should have been. The nurses took Richard out of the room, and my husband went with him. I fell asleep. When I woke, I was in the recovery ward with two nurses sitting at either side of my bed. They immediately wheeled me out of the room, down a long hall, and into another room where Richard and my husband were waiting. My medical team was gathered there as well. Everyone was crying. I drew near to his crib and met Richard for the first time.

He was already gone.

I didn't return to school for the remainder of the year. I didn't know how to go back. Was it even possible?

Days melted one into the next, and life became a hazy stream of sun, moon, sleep, visits from loved ones, and silence. I was home by myself, as my husband had to return to work, and without any sort of occupation, I realized that though I couldn't imagine ever moving past this, I couldn't bear to remain locked inside any longer. By the end of June, I allowed myself to be drawn like a magnet to the place I knew best.

I went to school.

It was summertime, so the custodial staff was up at the building every day, cleaning and refreshing the facilities for the academic year to come. That's what I did, too. I scraped gum off the undersides of desks, scrubbed out scuff marks from classroom floors, gathered trash, and deep-cleaned lockers. I didn't really know the maintenance team when I started helping out, but over the course of July and August, we developed relationships. They saw me as Jackie, not as a woman who just lost her baby. I didn't realize it at the time, but this interlude was invaluable in helping me relearn how to be around other people. Those staff members gently helped me reacclimate to being inside the school building, and the moments we laughed together and exchanged small talk loosened the terror that had unconsciously enclosed around my heart.

One day, as summer was nearing its end and the first day of school loomed ever larger, I ran into a student. It was Scott. We seemed to catch sight of each other at the same time from across the hall. I froze. What should I do? What could I do? He looked at me, and I could see the torrent of complex and impossible emotions cascading across his face.

"I don't know what to say," he told me.

"Neither do I." And then we were both crying.

"I can't believe what happened," he said. "It's made me question my faith. I had my church praying for you, and now..." He trailed off.

This was a conversation I wasn't ready for. It was a conversation I didn't want to have in the first place. But I wasn't alone in my pain. Talking to Scott helped me realize I wasn't facing any of this on my own.

As the next school year started, the students and staff at my school comforted me. Because of my slow, healing summer and unplanned encounter with Scott, I could turn and face the future. I was supported as I rose back up and looked a new year in the face. I could reconcile the parts of myself that were torn in two. I had left the year prior as a mother-to-be who was eager to introduce a new member into her family; I was returning by myself. Except, of course, that I wasn't by myself. As I came back to school, I was surrounded by a community of young people and colleagues who cared about me.

Though I've lost someone significant, and a part of me will always bear his memory and mark that loss, I now have more I can give. The paradox of grief.

Losing Richard has made me more empathetic and understanding. I see sorrow and struggle in my students' lives in a way I never could before. I'm more attuned to subtle changes in them, the almost unobservable shadows that flicker across their features. My eyes are open wider, and I'm so much more sensitive, equipped with an antenna that can filter through muddled noise to recognize rare frequencies of pain.

My students were a safe harbor for me when I was in the eye of a storm. Now, because of Richard, I'm grateful I have more capacity to be a safe place for them in return.

## Path into Education

I've always had a deep relationship with education and the academic life. As a student, I loved going to school every day. I loved learning and was eager to catch every drop of knowledge and information my teachers scattered throughout the day. As a teacher myself, that enthusiasm hasn't waned. I still venture through the school days discovering and changing in new ways. The difference now? The lessons come from my students.

I guess I could've been called a teacher's pet when I was young, but I knew I wanted to be an educator from the very beginning, and I did all I could to be close to my teachers, to watch them, to absorb their magic and methods, and to prepare myself to follow in their footsteps. I had especially exceptional English teachers my junior and senior years, and when I look back now, it's easy to see the course markers directing me toward education. I consider myself lucky to have known what I wanted from a young age. I was good at school and I enjoyed it. My line of thinking really was as a simple as "I excel at this, so I'll keep following it and see where it takes me." And it's taken me back to the start. Full circle.

When I have days I want to desert the profession, when I feel I've endured all I can and it seems the frustrations and red tape outweigh the rewards, I think of my students. I remember all they've done for me and all they've seen me through. It refocuses me. In the way that education has been a place of rest and safety for me, I aim to offer that same space to my students. I want that solace and comfort to be part of their experience, and if I can have a hand in giving shape to that reality, I will. They do the same for me.

It was a Thursday in the spring, and things just hadn't been falling my way. It had been one of those days in which things that usually are smooth and effortless turn stubborn and painstaking. There was no real cause for any of it. It just was. I looked forward to my prep period, an hour of quiet planning and energy conservation. And finally taking a bathroom break. I was sitting at my desk, pulling together some materials for an upcoming week of lessons, when one of my students, Shauna, rapped on the doorjamb. I knew she had been walking through some hard things personally, and I could read some of that weariness and sadness in her face.

"Mrs. Mancinelli?"

"Hey, Shauna. What's up?"

"Would it be okay if I sat in here during your plan? It's my study hall. I won't interrupt you. I just need a place to be." She scratched at the spine of the textbook she was holding in her arms.

"Sure," I said. "Have a seat wherever." I saw her relief and could relate. There had been a lot of times I didn't know where to go or what to do with myself, and I turned to school. Especially when I lost my son, Richard. I know how it feels to need a shelter and to find it inside a classroom.

Shauna and I worked independently, taking care of our tasks and responsibilities. Toward the end of the hour, I walked out of the room to pick up some copies from the office, and when I came back, she'd left already. I walked back to my desk and found a note with a message on it: *Thank you for letting me sit in here. It made my day so much better.*

That's it. In the midst of paperwork, meetings, bureaucracy, and mountains of grading, it is moments like this one that remind me why I choose education over and over. My kids are funny and fun and bright and kind. I really can't see myself doing anything else, and these relationships continue to buoy me against the frustrations threatening to take me under. I know what I'm doing is making a difference, even if it's just to one student, but beyond even that, it's making a difference to me.

I found my way to education when I entered it as a student, out of necessity. I stay because I can't get enough. I've received my bachelor's degree and my master's, and I racked up forty-something extra hours more than I needed. I love it! I love learning and the unpredictability of the classroom. For all the bad days and the hard moments, there are tenfold more good days and great moments. It's exciting to walk into my classroom and not know what awaits me. Every class, every hour, every student is a surprise. That keeps me focused and engaged and sharpens me in more ways than one.

Education is an endeavor that can take a lot from you. For educators, it can consume you completely if you let it. The emotional maintenance of students and parents, not to mention yourself, is exhausting. The hours are long and the work is meticulous, and no matter how hard you work, it will always feel like there is so much more to be done. But it gives so much back to you. When I miscarried two months into my time at a new school, it was there for me. When I didn't know what else to do or where to turn, I could turn to books and lesson plans and the familiar structures of education. When I lost Richard, my students and school community were there for me, helping me heal and recover and reaffirming the refuge I had always known school to be. Being with my kids is a balm and a joy. They fill me up. Yeah, it's hard work, but so worthwhile. The best things in life are the ones that require effort, and I wouldn't want to expend mine anywhere, or for the sake of anyone, else.

## Best Practice

*"For educators, [teaching] can consume you completely if you let it. The emotional maintenance of students and parents, not to mention yourself, is exhausting. The hours are long and the work is meticulous, and no matter how hard you work, it will always feel like there is so much more to be done."*

You can't do it all.

You can't do it *all.*

In education, every student has a unique set of needs you want to meet. There are innumerable opportunities to go the extra mile for every single one of them, but you begin each day with a finite amount of energy, resources, and time. Finding that mythical work-life balance creates space for you to replenish yourself, so you actually have a healthier, fuller approach to instruction. Not every lesson plan can be perfect. You can't save every student. Not every assignment needs to be graded before you leave the building. The goal should be to work smarter and more efficiently, not until you've depleted yourself entirely. Carving out time for rest and relaxation is not a guilty pleasure. You don't need to bring home the stress of ungraded assignments, unresolved student issues, or all the work left undone. Monitor your thoughts and rein them in when they threaten to get out of hand. Nonstop worrying won't make you a better teacher, but good sleep, personal fulfillment, and balance will.

Think about the work-related responsibilities and obligations that weigh on you most. What boundaries can you set for yourself that will help exchange your guilt for relief? Find a friend who can keep you in check when you're off the clock. Resolve to leave school by a certain time each day. Don't check your work email at home. Find non-negotiable activities that are restorative and invigorating, like walking your pet or cooking dinner with your spouse, and do them every day, no matter how far you've gotten in your work.

# Karen Workun

*Jenks, Oklahoma*

## Moment of Impact

I drove to school that morning like normal: thinking through the plan for that day's lesson, sorting through options and activities, discussion starters, homework, and so on. My thoughts were interrupted when I passed by a bad wreck on the highway that took me to work each day. My heart and prayers went out to those involved in the accident, only managing to think, "It'd be a miracle if anyone in that car made it out alive." And then my commute continued.

The morning went on as planned and by all accounts seemed typical. My lunch break, however, brought with it a cruel change. A small group of teachers, myself included, were called into the office for a brief meeting. That meeting ended up being about the wreck I had passed earlier that day and the people in the car. One in particular.

Sarah was a quiet, hardworking student and a sweet young lady. She kept largely to herself, but her faithful presence was a comfort to her classmates, and to me. Her smile was delicate and light and warmed those who came into her orbit. She was one of those diamond-in-the-rough kinds of students, and she was pregnant. In fact, just the day before, she brought her most recent sonogram images to school and gave me an update on her baby.

Sarah died in that car wreck.

My ears started ringing. It couldn't be true. The facts offered in that moment resounded like a hammer striking a bell over and over, filling the room with a deafening silence. We were told Sarah's boyfriend had picked her up, and they had taken the highway toward Yukon High School. The roads were unusually slick from the morning dew, which made the car slide, which led to Sarah and her baby departing from this life far too early.

The details of what happened were straightforward, but fitting those details into the framework of my mind seemed impossible. As the meeting drew near its close, the other teachers and I were reminded of the relentlessness of the school day. The bell was quickly bringing our next class and with it, students who needed to be taken care of. But what about us? Who would take care of us? And why weren't we able to take care of Sarah and her baby? We were told to remain quiet on the matter and only address direct questions with simple statements to prevent disruptive rumors from circulating.

My two classes after lunch came and went. In the busyness of the afternoon, my mind closed the door to that darkened room holding my chaotic thoughts of Sarah, her life, her death, and my clumsy attempt to make sense of it all. The final class of the day came to an end. The door closed behind my students. Everything was quiet. Heavy. Still. Without students, without distraction, and without comfort, I sat alone as that door within my mind opened.

I cried and cried, struggling for breath between sobs, grasping for any semblance of comfort and relief. Through my tears, I reached for the phone to call my husband. I needed someone to help me shoulder the weight of the sorrow I'd carried and concealed so quietly all day. The relief at hearing his voice was immediate.

Once my tears were spent and my mind had cleared, I thought of the prospect of tomorrow. Imagining myself standing in front of my first-hour class,

Sarah's seat empty again, I felt utterly helpless. I considered where to turn for more help, and I made the trip to our school's counseling office. I asked, "What should I do tomorrow?" After talking with one of our counselors, my heart began to settle. She explained to me the prevailing dynamics of a situation like the one we were facing. My students would be experiencing grief, and they needed to be assured that what they were feeling was valid and real. They would need space to process both the finality of life and the pain of losing a friend and classmate. In the end, the counselor offered to sit in on my class the next day to provide support for both my students and me. I gladly accepted, immeasurably relieved at not having to face my kids alone, again.

Although I was terribly unprepared for a situation of this complexity, I realized I was not alone. In reaching out to my husband and our school counselor, I shared a load I couldn't bear on my own. With some of that weight lifted, I was able to stand in front of my students and confront the reality of death alongside them, so we could share both our grief and our support.

Tragic moments, if navigated well, have the potential to create the most beautiful expressions of our humanity. In the midst of our sorrow that morning, and with the guidance of our school counselor, my students expressed their grief in touching and tangible ways.

Some wrote Sarah letters. Others printed out pictures of her to distribute around the school in remembrance of her life. Others simply wept. My job was to provide space for these young people to work their way through the moment.

Through Sarah's death, I learned a number of valuable lessons as a teacher. I learned that managing overwhelming situations, like this one, required me to give away my grief, my ego, and ultimately my control of the classroom. I tabled lesson plans indefinitely to give my students as much time as they needed to process their pain. I also gave up my place at the head of my classroom, so another professional could better lead. These changes were necessary for my class to survive in the face of our worst realities.

Sometimes, being an effective leader for your students means moving to the side and allowing someone else to assume your position up front. From this place, you can better walk with your students through life's challenges. In doing so, you will learn deeper truths about your profession, your life, and your students.

## Path into Education

*"You never really understand a person until you consider things from his point of view [...] until you climb into his skin and walk around in it." Atticus Finch,* To Kill a Mockingbird

Empathy. There is no disagreement you can't reconcile, no difference you can't equalize, if you're able to develop empathy for another person. And the very act of reading and engaging with literature is empathy in practice.

One of biggest reasons why I am an educator today is because I believe education is the most powerful vehicle for social change. It is the greatest tool we have at our disposal, the sharpest weapon we have to wield. The aim of education is not simply to go about daily work, take tests, receive grades, and move forward from one arbitrary level to the next. Real education, its underlying spirit, is a cultivation of the entire self and being informed about where that self fits into the whole of society.

As a teacher, I encourage my students to lean fully into who they are. I try to set this example in my classroom. As I share parts of my life, I invite them into my story. They, in turn, invite me into theirs. Revealing to them who I am, telling personal anecdotes about trivial successes or significant challenges—everything from a kitchen mishap while making last night's dinner to the triumphant completion of a book that's taken me too long to read—peels back some of my layers and allows my students to see me as a human rather than just an adult who materializes in the classroom every morning and then *poof* disappears after the final bell each day.

I consider my relationships with students to be mutual partnerships. Our worth and dignity are equal, though we have different roles in the classroom, but getting to this place requires respecting and understanding each other and having an awareness of what we're all going through. I learned this lesson as a student myself.

When I was in high school, I saw the effects of prejudice and closed-mindedness firsthand. There were some Black students in my school who were widely beloved, popular, sociable, and fun to be around. Everyone enjoyed their presence at school and loved to hang out with them and learn from them in class.

That's what I thought, at least. That's what most of us thought. Until they received death threats that drove them to leave my high school.

These students who were so admired by most of us were victimized by a few intimidators so insecure and ignorant they permitted themselves to articulate their deepest darkness. They were so uninterested in getting to know my wonderful classmates and "walk around in their skin," as Atticus would say, so incapable of fathoming an experience outside of their own, that they pushed them away. And it's this—the inability to understand or even entertain lifestyles, opinions, and motivations different from our own—that creates loss. Not for one but for all.

As a student, part of my response to the situation was to form a Multi-Cultural Club, an on-campus group celebrating diversity and seeking to bridge the gaps between our differences rather than let them separate us even further. This is something I believed our student body needed and something I wanted to do, but I wouldn't have been brave or bold enough to do it without a teacher championing me and my efforts.

Mrs. Romano was my AP Literature teacher. The works we read in her class were all about challenging our existing worldviews. Getting into the minds of characters like the narrator from *Invisible Man* and seeing their struggles invited all of us to step into an attitude of empathy and compassion. Mrs. Romano wanted us to understand everyone's place in society, appreciate all of their unique dilemmas, and be willing to act on behalf of their interests, not just our own.

She became the sponsor of the Multi-Cultural Club. Because we shared the same perspective on what we believed the school and its students needed. Because we wanted to expand those perspectives and provide that same sharpening opportunity to others. We saw the injustice perpetrated against those students, against our fellow humans, and we decided to do something about it. Much like Atticus.

I am a teacher because I want to continue to fight against small-mindedness, and I use literature and education to do it. I want to be the cheerleader for my students that Mrs. Romano was for me. I want to help advocate for those whose points of view often go unappreciated, underestimated, unacknowledged, or are misunderstood entirely. I want to expose students to unlikable characters, moral dilemmas, and complicated conflicts through literature so that they're equipped to handle them off the page.

Education is the key to building a better world. It's the foundation of a more empathetic electorate. It's the touchstone of a healthy society. By reading the stories of others, whether fictional or not, we can step into their shoes and walk around in them for a bit. Only then can we hope for a society of understanding and compassion. Only then can we invite them into our own shoes and, more importantly, our own stories.

## Best Practice

*"There was no way I could have planned for or anticipated all of the complexities of a situation like [a student's death] arising. One of the best things you can do when you're working in the school environment is to know your building, know your people, and know your resources. So I went to our counselor and just said, 'What should I do tomorrow?' I had Sarah first hour, so it was going to be the first class of the day. She agreed to come in and sit with the class, so I had a professional in there with me to help me navigate that, and I learned so much from her that morning and from how she interacted with the students."*

When hard challenges arise, you won't have all the answers, and you aren't expected to handle them all on your own. Teachers and other educational professionals are asked to take on a number of responsibilities that sap them of energy, physically and emotionally. And life in the classroom every day is hard. Unexpected moments arise, and occasionally, so do tragedies, like the death of a student, staff member, or other loved one of the student body. When these things happen, utilize the resources around you.

When Karen lost her student, Sarah, she was unprepared for the impact that loss would have not only on her students but also on her personally. No one can be adequately prepared for such a heartbreaking incident. Karen recognized this and sought help and support from others, reaching out to her husband for comfort and her school counselor for in-classroom assistance.

Know the professionals in your building, like counselors, who can come alongside you and your students in difficult times. Don't hesitate to reach out for help and bring in necessary outside support. If you don't know who the point people are at your site, find out. Explore opportunities and organizations in your area that can provide further aid. Get familiar with your local resources for grief counseling and trauma support. Unfortunately, you never know when you may need to take advantage of them.

# Anna Fusco

*Broward County, Florida*

## Next Steps

**B**eing an educator isn't what it used to be.

Educators used to be universally respected. To dedicate one's life to the education and improvement of young people used to be seen as a noble profession. Everyone could agree that teaching was important, urgent, and dignified. Teachers were portrayed in the media as pillars of morality and integrity, even beloved. The sentimental ephemera of the classroom were cozy and familiar sights: apples, rulers, blackboards. Now, the public's view of educators and our profession is a little different.

When I was a student, I had an exemplary teacher who inspired me to follow her path into education. Ms. Helms was my middle-school P.E. teacher and she was tough as nails. She cared about her students, though, and you could tell. We respected her and we knew she wanted our best and would accept nothing less. She helped me learn that doing the right thing actually does make a difference and will yield a good outcome. The world we live in now doesn't necessarily corroborate that idea, but Ms. Helms showed me that sticking up for the underdog and fighting against injustice is important work that can't be stopped. Because of her, I declared physical education as my major in college. She's also the godmother of my son. Her strength and gumption inspired me to carry on her legacy as an educator and to fight the good fight on behalf of students. This sort of advocacy and watchfulness is especially needed in today's educational landscape.

Schools have become battlegrounds. Classrooms are the chosen contexts for government leaders and officials to test their political ideas and issues. As the world around us grows more and more uncontrollable and unpredictable, restrictions within our nation's schools increase. People fear what's coming next. They're afraid of the unfamiliar and the unknown, and in reaction to those feelings, they interrogate the expertise of educators, school districts, and statewide curricula. Over the course of the pandemic, educators transformed (not for the first time) from heroes to villains as the unbearable and fatiguing demands of pandemic protocols wore down teachers, students, their families, and the general public. The political and social upheaval occurring in our society has disoriented people, so they look to a scapegoat. They look to something they can control and change, a place they perceive as the origin point of the issues they currently face. They undermine and hogtie educators, telling these trained professionals what they can and cannot do.

Being in education isn't what it used to be.

But you've just read countless stories from remarkable educators who have walked challenging paths, navigated unthinkable obstacles, and reaped invaluable benefits. We know this profession is noble indeed. It is important and urgent, more so now than it ever was. We recognize that the profession is being altered from the outside, but there are concrete, practical ways we can protect and shape it from the inside.

Investigate. The inundation of "news" via today's social media is nearly inescapable. With that, there is a lot of room for truth and falsehood to muddle together. Do research and resolve to consume verified information from a diverse array of unbiased, trustworthy sources. Present those same kinds of sources to your students. Ignore the false narratives that pervade culture. Remember that education is crucial to the functioning of a healthy, balanced, developed society, and without equitable educational opportunities for all citizens—and informed, passionate, qualified educators—that society ceases to be.

Participate. Learn about and become involved in organizations dedicated to raising awareness around issues that affect education, our students, and our communities. Find and join your local teachers' union, and if there isn't one in your area, consider creating one. Stay plugged into your subject area and remain on the cutting edge of new research, pedagogy, and instructional strategies. Collaborate with other educators and support each other. Be a sounding board for one another and encourage each other that no one is isolated in the challenges and feelings they're experiencing. We are stronger together, and when we work together across lines of difference, real change can and does happen.

Advocate. Remember that the role of educator is an honor and a privilege. We possess true influence over our students, and we can make a difference in their lives. It's a position to take seriously, and it's the starting line for instilling self-worth in our students, showing them the equal value of every human's rights and dignity, and building the traits of empathy, compassion, and independence. As educators, it's neither our place nor our job to impose our morals and values on others, but we should impose on them the values of kindness and decency. We should demonstrate these qualities to our students and encourage our students to show them to each other. Through these relationships, we can chip away at the terror and constriction of society one conversation at a time. That work begins in the classroom beside our students.

As the president of the Broward County teachers' union, I spend a lot of time in the area's school buildings. One of those schools is Marjory Stoneman Douglas High School where, in 2018, fourteen students and three staff members were killed during a school shooting. Every time I step foot on that campus, I get weak in the knees. These tragic events, and they continue to happen over and over again, bring a lot of things to the surface of our collective consciousness. For me, one of those things is the imperative to fight for the students and staff in my county. The work educators do matters more than we think. There is inherent risk in entering school buildings each day, yet we do it because the students and their futures are more than worth it.

Education is not what it once was, but its value and importance has only increased. It is the first line of defense and development of free thought, intellectual curiosity, social-emotional intelligence, and human dignity and respect. So do all you can to further that work, to never give up, and to stay vigilant.

Remember your students and all the potential they possess.

Remember we're taking steps to create the society and world we want to live in.

Remember you're not alone.

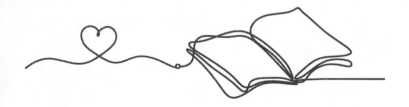

# Acknowledgments

This project would not exist if it weren't for the educators who graciously and selflessly trusted us with their stories. We are indebted to you not only for your candor but also for your daily sacrifice in classrooms across the country.

Thank you to Morgan James Publishing and all those there who joined our team as champions of this project, in particular Emily Madison.

To Erin and Katie with Relate Then Educate: your efforts and passion activate the potency of this book and carry this mission forward every day.

To Adam and Darla: we are grateful for your forbearance, patience, and encouragement. Thank you for keeping us grounded. We love you.

And finally, to every educator past, present, and future: this world is hopeless without you. Keep at it.

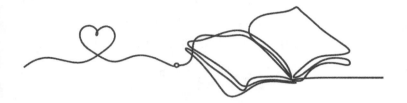

# About the Authors

Rick Holmes is a former secondary school teacher and coach. With over two decades of classroom experience, Rick uses his perspective and experience to amplify the voices of classroom teachers through Relate Then Educate. He has a bachelor's degree in secondary education from Oklahoma State University, a master's degree in school counseling from Lamar

University, and is the son of two lifetime educators who proudly served their community for over eighty years combined. He lives in Tulsa, Oklahoma, with his family.

Andrea Avey is a former educator who landed in the classroom by way of Teach for America. She studied English and Spanish at Oklahoma State University and holds an MA in humanities from the University of Chicago. She lives in Chicago with her husband and their dog, Fitzgerald.

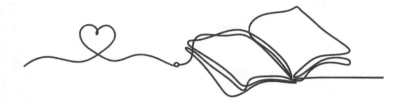

# Additional Resources

To contact Relate Then Educate for professional development, author engagements, and more, visit our website: www.relatetheneducate.com

**Arturo Aviña**
Los Angeles, California
Theatre, elementary
@schooledbyarturo

**Justin Belt**
Carrollton, Texas
English, high school
@_jbspeaks

**Tonya Bobo**
North Little Rock, Arkansas
Kindergarten

**Amy Crawford**
Maryville, Tennessee
English, seventh grade
@reachthemtoteachthem

**Roxana Dueñas**
Los Angeles, California
History, ninth grade

**Abby French**
Shenandoah County, Virginia
History, sixth grade
@awfrench1

**Anna Fusco**
Broward County, Florida
President, Broward County Teacher Union
@afusco_BTU

**Lorena Lopez**
Hammond, Indiana
English Language Learning

**Jackie Mancinelli**
Eastern Regional High School
Voorhees Township, New Jersey
English & English as a Second Language, high school
@starthealingtogether

**Carmelita "Carm" Shouldis**
Sicangu Community Development Corporation
Mission, South Dakota
First grade

**Pam Swan**
Greensboro, North Carolina
Second grade
@pammieswan

**Shelly Swisher**
Mesa, Arizona
English, high school

**Monte Syrie**
Cheney, Washington
English Language Arts, high school
@MonteSyrie

**Rachel Whalen**
Montpelier, Vermont
Kindergarten
@Rachwhalen

**Kelli Wilson**
Tulsa, Oklahoma
Counselor

**Karen Workun**
Jenks, Oklahoma
English, high school
@karenworkun

# A free ebook edition is available with the purchase of this book.

**To claim your free ebook edition:**

1. Visit MorganJamesBOGO.com
2. Sign your name CLEARLY in the space
3. Complete the form and submit a photo of the entire copyright page
4. You or your friend can download the ebook to your preferred device

## Print & Digital Together Forever.

Snap a photo

Free ebook

Read anywhere

Printed in the USA
CPSIA information can be obtained
at www.ICGtesting.com
JSHW021910301023
51111JS00006B/66